Geography

for Cambridge IGCSE™ and O Level

EXAM PREPARATION AND PRACTICE

Helen Young & James Hickman

with Digital access

Shaftesbury Road, Cambridge CB2 8EA, United Kingdom

One Liberty Plaza, 20th Floor, New York, NY 10006, USA

477 Williamstown Road, Port Melbourne, VIC 3207, Australia

314–321, 3rd Floor, Plot 3, Splendor Forum, Jasola District Centre, New Delhi – 110025, India

103 Penang Road, #05–06/07, Visioncrest Commercial, Singapore 238467

Cambridge University Press & Assessment is a department of the University of Cambridge.

We share the University's mission to contribute to society through the pursuit of education, learning and research at the highest international levels of excellence.

www.cambridge.org
Information on this title: www.cambridge.org/9781009818315

First published 2026
20 19 18 17 16 15 14 13 12 11 10 9 8 7 6 5 4 3 2 1

Printed in the Netherlands by Wilco

A catalogue record for this publication is available from the British Library

ISBN   978-1-009-81831-5   Exam Preparation and Practice Print with digital access
ISBN   978-1-009-81832-2   Digital Exam Preparation and Practice
ISBN   978-1-009-81830-8   Exam Preparation and Practice eBook

Additional resources for this publication at www.cambridge.org/go

For EU product safety concerns, contact us at Calle de José Abascal, 56, 1°, 28003 Madrid, Spain, or email eugpsr@cambridge.org.

2025 Cambridge Dedicated Teacher Awards

Our **Cambridge Dedicated Teacher Awards** are an opportunity to show appreciation for the incredible work teachers do every day.

Thank you to everyone who nominated this year; we have been inspired and moved by all of your stories. Well done to all of our nominees for your dedication to learning and for inspiring the next generation of thinkers, leaders and innovators.

Congratulations to our winners!

Global Winner

Sub-Saharan Africa

Portia Dzilah
Pakro-Adjinase St. James Anglican Basic School, Ghana

East Asia

Yun Xie
Yew Wah International Education School of Shanghai Lingang, China

Europe

Oleksandr Zhuk
Zaporizhzhia Special Comprehensive Boarding Xchool, Dzherelo, Ukraine

Latin America

Eduardo Pérez
Instituto Técnico Guaimaral, Colombia

North America

Isabel de Feria
Marjory Stoneman Douglas Elementary, USA

Middle East and North Africa

Farrukh Saleem
Pakistan International School Jeddah English Section, Saudi Arabia

Pakistan

Adnan Ahmed Usmani
Bahria Town School and College, Pakistan

South Asia

Sakina Bharmal
The Galaxy School - Wadi, India

Southeast Asia & Pacific

Polly Neville
Denla British School Bangkok, Thailand

For more information about our dedicated teachers and their stories, go to **dedicatedteacher.cambridge.org**

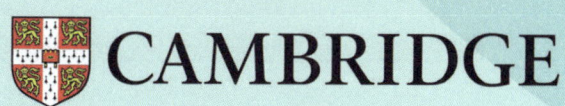

CAMBRIDGE

Contents

Extra digital questions for all topics can be found online at Cambridge GO.
For more information on how to access and use your digital resource,
please see inside front cover.

› How to use this series

This suite of resources supports students and teachers following the Cambridge IGCSE™, IGCSE (9-1) and O Level Geography syllabuses (0460/0976/2217) for examination from 2027. The components in the series are designed to work together and help students develop the necessary knowledge and skills for studying Geography.

The Coursebook is designed for students to use in class with guidance from the teacher. It offers full coverage of the Cambridge IGCSE™, IGCSE (9-1) and O Level Geography syllabuses. Each topic contains explanations, definitions, a variety of tasks and detailed specific examples with questions to engage students and develop their geographical skills.

The Teacher's Resource is the foundation of this series. It offers inspiring ideas about how to teach this course including teaching notes, how to avoid common misconceptions, suggestions for differentiation, formative assessment and language support, answers and extra materials such as worksheets and end-of-topic tests.

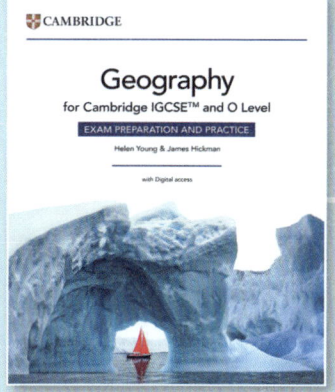

The Exam Preparation and Practice* provides dedicated support for students in preparing for their final assessments. The resource includes hundreds of knowledge recall questions, a checklist of exam skills with corresponding questions, past paper question practice, and reflection features. This resource should be used alongside the Coursebook, so students can most effectively increase their confidence and readiness for their exams.

*This text has not been through the endorsement process for the Cambridge Pathway. Any references or materials related to answers, grades, papers or examinations are based on the opinion of the author(s). The Cambridge International Education syllabus assessment guidance material and specimen papers should always be referred to for definitive guidance.

> How to use this book

This book will help you to check that you **know** the content of the syllabus and practise how to **show** this understanding in an exam. It will also help you be cognitively prepared and in the **flow**, ready for your exam. Research has shown that it is important that you do all three of these things, so we have designed the Know, Show, Flow approach to help you prepare effectively for exams.

Know	You will need to consolidate and then recall a lot of syllabus content.

Show	You should demonstrate your knowledge in the context of a Cambridge exam.

Flow	You should be cognitively engaged and ready to learn. This means reducing test anxiety.

Exam skills checklist

Category	Exam skill
Understanding the question	Recognise different question types
	Understand command words
	Mark scheme awareness
Providing an appropriate response	Understand connections between concepts
	Keep to time
	Know what a good answer looks like
Developing supportive behaviours	Reflect on progress
	Manage test anxiety

This **Exam skills checklist** helps you to develop the awareness, behaviours and habits that will support you when revising and preparing for your exams. For more exam skills advice, including understanding command words and managing your time effectively, please go to the **Exam skills chapter**.

Know

The full syllabus content of your IGCSE, IGCSE (9-1) and O Level Geography course is covered in your Cambridge coursebook. This book will provide you with different types of questions to support you as you prepare for your exams. You will answer **Knowledge recall questions** that are designed to make sure you understand a topic, and **Recall and connect questions** to help you recall past learning and connect different concepts.

KNOWLEDGE FOCUS

Knowledge focus boxes summarise the content that you will answer questions on in each topic of this book. You can refer back to your Cambridge coursebook to remind yourself of the full detail of the syllabus content.

Knowledge recall question

Testing yourself is a good way to check that your understanding is secure. These questions will help you to recall the core knowledge you have acquired during your course, and highlight any areas where you may need more practice. They are indicated with a blue bar with a gap, at the side of the page. We recommend that you answer the Knowledge recall questions just after you have covered the relevant topic in class, and then return to them at a later point to check you have properly understood the content.

≪ RECALL AND CONNECT 1 ≪

To consolidate your learning, you need to test your memory frequently. These questions will test that you remember what you learned in other topics, in addition to what you are practising in the current topic.

UNDERSTAND THESE TERMS

These list the important vocabulary that you should understand for each topic. Definitions are provided in the glossary of your Cambridge coursebook.

Show

Exam questions test specific knowledge, skills and understanding. You need to be prepared so that you have the best opportunity to show what you know in the time you have during the exam. In addition to practising recall of the syllabus content, it is important to build your exam skills throughout the year.

EXAM SKILLS FOCUS

This feature outlines the exam skills you will practise in each topic, alongside the Knowledge focus. They are drawn from the core set of eight exam skills, listed in the exam skills checklist. You will practise specific exam skills, such as understanding command words, within each topic. More general exam skills, such as managing text anxiety, are covered in the Exam skills chapter.

Exam skills question

These questions will help you to develop your exam skills and demonstrate your understanding. To help you become familiar with exam-style questioning, these questions follow the style and use the language of real exam questions, and have allocated marks. They are indicated with a solid red bar at the side of the page.

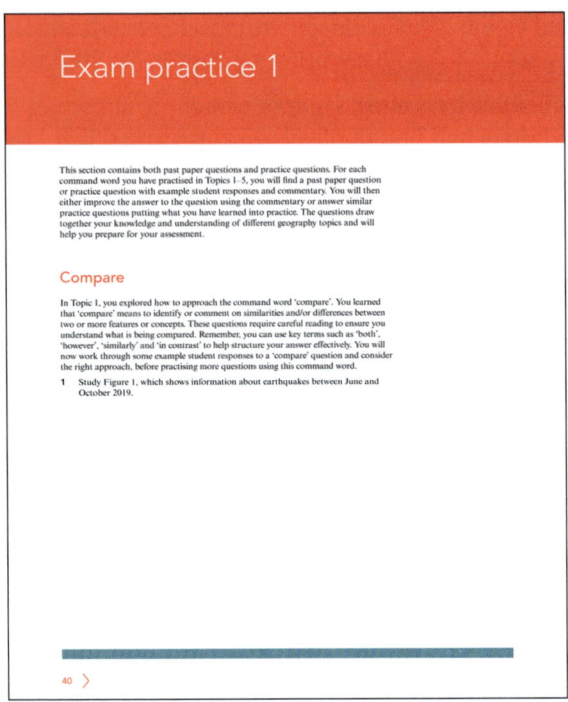

Looking at sample answers to past paper questions helps you to understand what to aim for.

The **Exam practice** sections in this resource contain example student responses and examiner-style commentary showing how the answer could be improved (both written by the authors).

Flow

Preparing for exams can be stressful. One of the approaches recommended by educational psychologists to help with this stress is to improve behaviours around exam preparation. This involves testing yourself in manageable chunks, accompanied by self-evaluation. You should avoid cramming, and build in more preparation time. This book is structured to help you do this.

REFLECTION

This feature asks you to think about the approach that you take to your exam preparation, and how you might improve this in the future. Reflecting on how you plan, monitor and evaluate your revision and preparation will help you to do your best in your exams.

SELF-ASSESSMENT CHECKLIST

These checklists return to the Learning intentions from your Coursebook, as well as the Exam skills focus boxes from each topic. The statements that relate to Exam skills are indicated with a solid red bar at the side of the page. Checking in on how confident you feel in each of these areas will help you to focus your exam preparation. The 'Show it' prompts will allow you to test your rating. You should revisit any areas that you rate 'Needs more work' or 'Almost there'.

Now I can	Show it	Needs more work	Almost there	Confident to move on

Increasing your ability to recognise the signs of exam-related stress and working through some techniques for how to cope with it will help to make your exam preparation manageable. The **Exam skills chapter** will support you with this.

If a question asks you to complete a diagram or graph, you can find a printable copy of this in the Topic Resource Sheet and Past Paper Questions Resource Sheet, which are available to download from Cambridge GO.

Digital questions

Extra digital questions, in the form of **Multiple choice** and **Flip cards**, for all chapters can be found online at Cambridge GO. For more information on how to access and use your digital resource, please see inside the front cover.

- Provides lots of additional practice to reinforce knowledge and understanding
- Gives instant feedback to support autonomy over your own learning
- Encourages self-assessment to understand your strengths and weaknesses
- User-friendly design to help with easy navigation

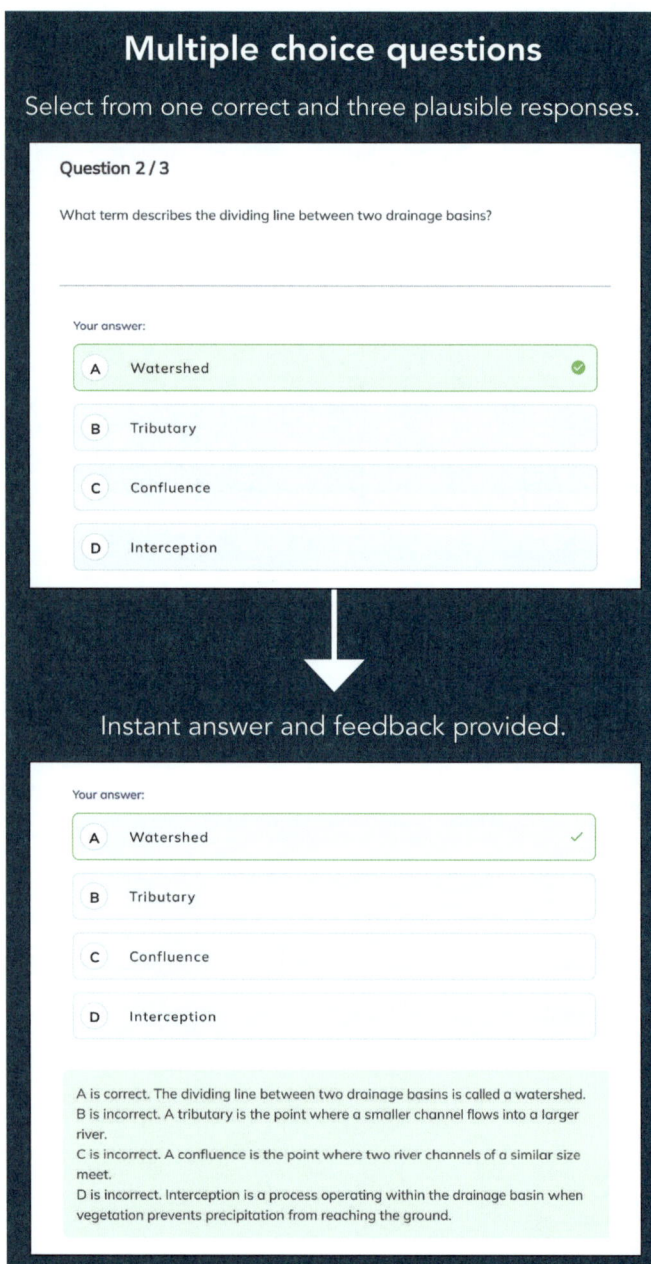

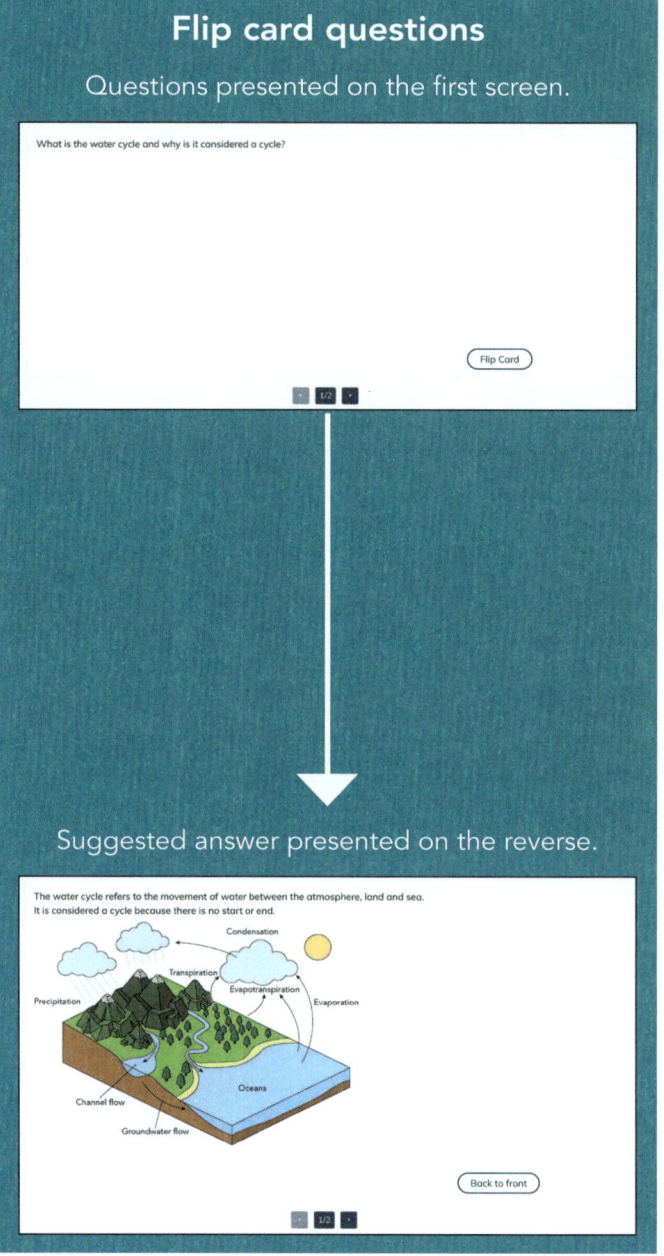

Syllabus assessment objectives for IGCSE and O Level Geography

You should be familiar with the Assessment Objectives from the syllabus, as you will need to show evidence of these requirements in your responses.

The assessment objectives for this syllabus are:

Assessment objective	Paper 1	Paper 2	Component 3 or Paper 4
AO1: Knowledge and understanding	37%	37%	20%
AO2: Skills and analysis	43%	43%	60%
AO3: Evaluation and decision-making	20%	20%	20%

Exam skills

by Lucy Parsons

What's the point of this book?

Most students make one really basic mistake when they're preparing for exams. What is it? It's focusing far too much on learning 'stuff' – that's facts, figures, ideas, information – and not nearly enough time practising exam skills.

The students who work really, really hard but are disappointed with their results are nearly always students who focus on memorising stuff. They think to themselves, 'I'll do practice papers once I've revised everything.' The trouble is, they start doing practice papers too late to really develop and improve how they communicate what they know.

What could they do differently?

When your final exam script is assessed, it should contain specific language, information and thinking skills in your answers. If you read a question in an exam and you have no idea what you need to do to give a good answer, the likelihood is that your answer won't be as brilliant as it could be. That means your grade won't reflect the hard work you've put into revising for the exam.

There are different types of questions used in exams to assess different skills. You need to know how to recognise these question types and understand what you need to show in your answers.

So, how do you understand what to do in each question type?

That's what this book is all about. But first a little background.

Meet Benjamin Bloom

The psychologist Benjamin Bloom developed a way of classifying and valuing different skills we use when we learn, such as analysis and recalling information. We call these thinking skills. It's known as Bloom's Taxonomy and it's what most exam questions are based around.

If you understand Bloom's Taxonomy, you can understand what any type of question requires you to do. So, what does it look like?

Bloom's Taxonomy of thinking skills

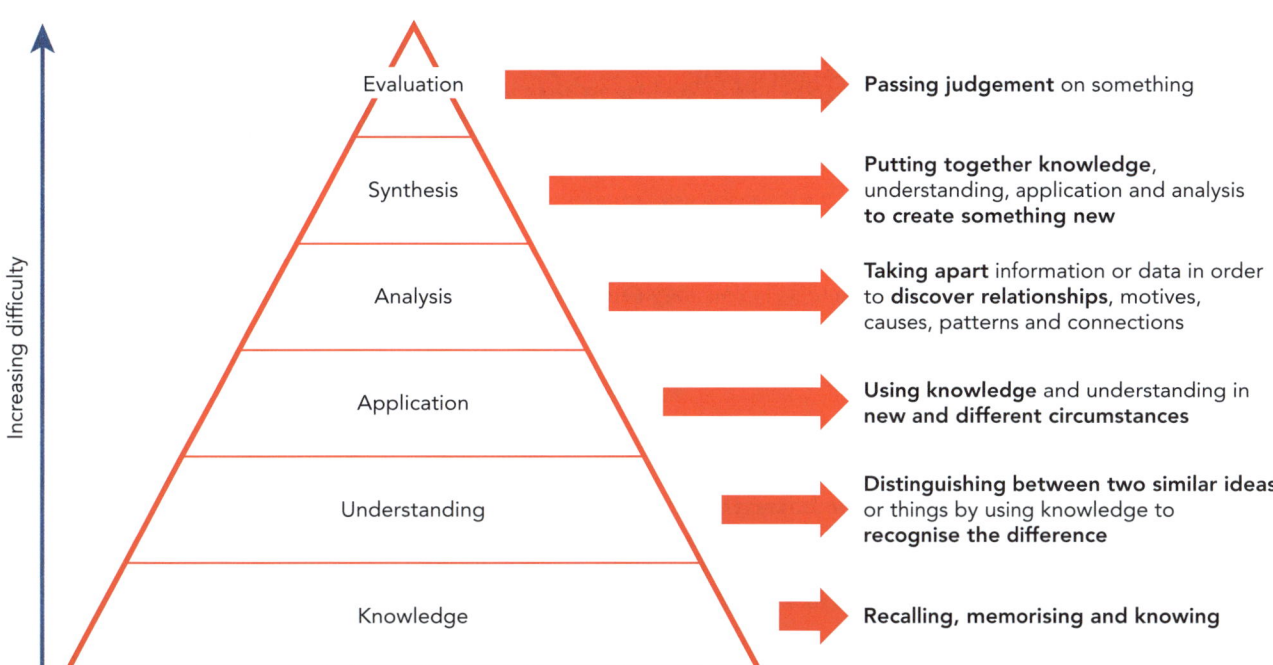

The key things to take away from this diagram are:

- Knowledge and understanding are known as lower-level thinking skills. They are less difficult than the other thinking skills. Exam questions that just test you on what you know are usually worth the lowest number of marks.

- All the other thinking skills are worth higher numbers of marks in exam questions. These questions need you to have some foundational knowledge and understanding but are far more about how you think than what you know. They involve:

  - Taking what you know and using it in unfamiliar situations (application).

  - Going deeper into information to discover relationships, motives, causes, patterns and connections (analysis).

  - Using what you know and think to create something new – whether that's an essay, long-answer exam question, a solution to a maths problem or a piece of art (synthesis).

  - Assessing the value of something, e.g. the reliability of the results of a scientific experiment (evaluation).

In this introductory chapter, you'll be shown how to develop the skills that enable you to communicate what you know and how you think. This will help you achieve to the best of your abilities. In the rest of the book, you'll have a chance to practise these exam skills by understanding how questions work and understanding what you need to show in your answers.

Every time you pick up this book and do a few questions, you're getting closer to achieving your dream results. So, let's get started!

Exam preparation and revision skills

What is revision?

If you think about it, the word 'revision' has two parts to it:

- re – which means 'again'

- vision – which is about seeing.

So, revision is literally about 'seeing again'. This means you're looking at something that you've already learned.

Typically, a teacher will teach you something in class. You may then do some questions on it, write about it in some way, or even do a presentation. You might then have an end-of-topic test sometime later. To prepare for this test, you need to 'look again' or revise what you were originally taught.

Step 1: Making knowledge stick

Every time you come back to something you've learned or revised you're improving your understanding and memory of that particular piece of knowledge. This is called **spaced retrieval**. This is how human memory works. If you don't use a piece of knowledge by recalling it, you lose it.

Everything we learn has to be physically stored in our brains by creating neural connections – joining brain cells together. The more often we 'retrieve' or recall a particular piece of knowledge, the stronger the neural connection gets. It's like lifting weights – the more often you lift, the stronger you get.

However, if you don't use a piece of knowledge for a long time, your brain wants to recycle the brain cells and use them for another purpose. The neural connections get weaker until they finally break, and the memory has gone. This is why it's really important to return often to things that you've learned in the past.

Great ways of doing this in your revision include:

- Testing yourself using flip cards – use the ones available in the digital resources for this book.

- Testing yourself (or getting someone else to test you) using questions you've created about the topic.

- Checking your recall of previous topics by answering the Recall and connect questions in this book.

- Blurting – writing everything you can remember about a topic on a piece of paper in one colour. Then, checking what you missed out and filling it in with another colour. You can do this over and over again until you feel confident that you remember everything.

- Answering practice questions – use the ones in this book.

- Getting a good night's sleep to help consolidate your learning.

> **The importance of sleep and creating long-term memory**
>
> When you go to sleep at night, your brain goes through an important process of taking information from your short-term memory and storing it in your long-term memory.
>
> This means that getting a good night's sleep is a very important part of revision. If you don't get enough good quality sleep, you'll actually be making your revision much, much harder.

Step 2: Developing your exam skills

We've already talked about the importance of exam skills, and how many students neglect them because they're worried about covering all the knowledge.

What actually works best is developing your exam skills at the same time as learning the knowledge.

What does this look like in your studies?

- Learning something at school and your teacher setting you questions from this book or from past papers. This tests your recall as well as developing your exam skills.

- Choosing a topic to revise, learning the content and then choosing some questions from this book to test yourself at the same time as developing your exam skills.

The reason why practising your exam skills is so important is that it helps you to get good at communicating what you know and what you think. The more often you do that, the more fluent you'll become in showing what you know in your answers.

Step 3: Getting feedback

The final step is to get feedback on your work.

If you're testing yourself, the feedback is what you got wrong or what you forgot. This means you then need to go back to those things to remind yourself or improve your understanding. Then, you can test yourself again and get more feedback. You can also congratulate yourself for the things you got right – it's important to celebrate any success, big or small.

If you're doing past paper questions or the practice questions in this book, you will need to mark your work. Marking your work is one of the most important things you can do to improve. It's possible to make significant improvements in your marks in a very short space of time when you start marking your work.

Why is marking your own work so powerful? It's because it teaches you to identify the strengths and weaknesses of your own work. When you look at the mark scheme and see how it's structured, you will understand what is needed in your answers to get the results you want.

This doesn't just apply to the knowledge you demonstrate in your answers. It also applies to the language you use and whether it's appropriately subject-specific, the structure of your answer, how you present it on the page and many other factors. Understanding, practising and improving on these things are transformative for your results.

The most important thing about revision

The most important way to make your revision successful is to make it active.

Sometimes, students say they're revising when they sit staring at their textbook or notes for hours at a time. However, this is a really ineffective way to revise because it's passive. In order to make knowledge and skills stick, you need to be doing something like the suggestions in the following diagram. That's why testing yourself and pushing yourself to answer questions that test higher-level thinking skills are so effective. At times, you might actually be able to feel the physical changes happening in your brain as you develop this new knowledge and these new skills. That doesn't come about without effort.

The important thing to remember is that while active revision feels much more like hard work than passive revision, you don't actually need to do nearly as much of it. That's because you remember knowledge and skills when you use active revision. When you use passive revision, it is much, much harder for the knowledge and skills to stick in your memory.

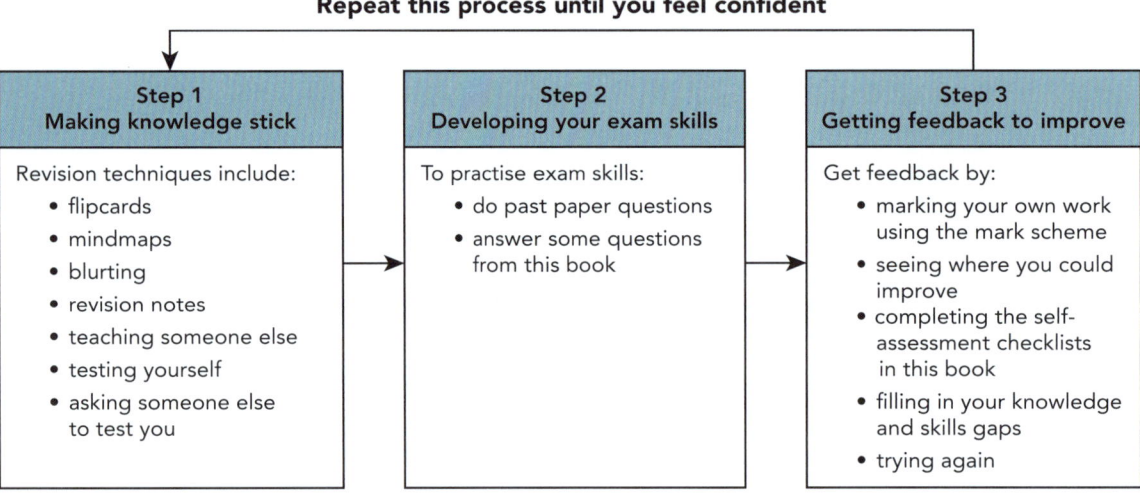

Repeat this process until you feel confident

Step 1 Making knowledge stick	Step 2 Developing your exam skills	Step 3 Getting feedback to improve
Revision techniques include: • flipcards • mindmaps • blurting • revision notes • teaching someone else • testing yourself • asking someone else to test you	To practise exam skills: • do past paper questions • answer some questions from this book	Get feedback by: • marking your own work using the mark scheme • seeing where you could improve • completing the self-assessment checklists in this book • filling in your knowledge and skills gaps • trying again

How to improve your exam skills

This book helps you to improve in eight different areas of exam skills, which are divided across three categories. These skills are highlighted in this book in the Exam skills focus at the start of each chapter and developed throughout the book using targeted questions, advice and reflections.

1   **Understand the questions: what are you being asked to do?**

   •   Know your question types.

   •   Understand command words.

   •   Work with mark scheme awareness.

2   **How to answer questions brilliantly**

   •   Understand connections between concepts.

   •   Keep to time.

   •   Know what a good answer looks like.

3   **Give yourself the best chance of success**

   •   Reflection on progress.

   •   How to manage test anxiety.

Understand the questions: what are you being asked to do?

Know your question types

In any exam, there will be a range of different question types. These different question types will test different types of thinking skills from Bloom's Taxonomy.

It is very important that you learn to recognise different question types. If you do lots of past papers, over time you will begin to recognise the structure of the paper for each of your subjects. You will know which types of questions may come first and which ones are more likely to come at the end of the paper. You can also complete past paper questions in the Exam practice sections in this book for additional practice.

You will also recognise the differences between questions worth a lower number of marks and questions worth more marks. The key differences are:

* how much you will need to write in your answer
* how sophisticated your answer needs to be in terms of the detail you give and the depth of thinking you show.

Types of questions

1   Multiple-choice questions

Multiple-choice questions are generally worth smaller numbers of marks. You will be given several possible answers to the question, and you will have to work out which one is correct using your knowledge and skills.

There is a chance of you getting the right answer with multiple-choice questions even if you don't know the answer. This is why you must **always give an answer for multiple-choice questions** as it means there is a chance you will earn the mark.

Multiple-choice questions are often harder than they appear. The possible answers can be very similar to each other. This means you must be confident in how you work out answers or have a high level of understanding to tell the difference between the possible answers.

Being confident in your subject knowledge and doing lots of practice multiple-choice questions will set you up for success. Use the resources in this book and the accompanying online resources to build your confidence.

This example of a multiple-choice question is worth one mark. You can see that all the answers have one part in common with at least one other answer. For example, palisade cells is included in three of the possible answers. That's why you have to really know the detail of your content knowledge to do well with multiple-choice questions.

Which two types of cells are found in plant leaves?

A   Palisade mesophyll and stomata
B   Palisade mesophyll and root hair
C   Stomata and chloroplast
D   Chloroplast and palisade mesophyll

2   **Questions requiring longer-form answers**

Questions requiring longer-form answers need you to write out your answer yourself.

With these questions, take careful note of how many marks are available and how much space you've been given for your answer. These two things will give you a good idea about how much you should say and how much time you should spend on the question.

A rough rule to follow is to write one sentence, or make one point, for each mark that is available. You will get better and better at these longer form questions the more you practise them.

In this example of a history question, you can see it is worth four marks. It is not asking for an explanation, just for you to list Lloyd George's aims. Therefore, you need to make four correct points in order to get full marks.

What were Lloyd George's aims during negotiations leading to the Treaty of Versailles?   [4]

3   **Essay questions**

Essay questions are the longest questions you will be asked to answer in an exam. They examine the higher-order thinking skills from Bloom's Taxonomy such as analysis, synthesis and evaluation.

To do well in essay questions, you need to talk about what you know, giving your opinion, comparing one concept or example to another, and evaluating your own ideas or the ones you're discussing in your answer.

You also need to have a strong structure and logical argument that guides the reader through your thought process. This usually means having an introduction, some main body paragraphs that discuss one point at a time, and a conclusion.

Essay questions are usually level-marked. This means that you don't get one mark per point you make. Instead, you're given marks for the quality of the ideas you're sharing as well as how well you present those ideas through the subject-specific language you use and the structure of your essay.

Practising essays and becoming familiar with the mark scheme is the only way to get really good at them.

Understand command words

What are command words?

Command words are the most important words in every exam question. This is because command words tell you what you need to do in your answer. Do you remember Bloom's Taxonomy? Command words tell you which thinking skill you need to demonstrate in the answer to each question.

Two very common command words are **describe** and **explain**.

When you see the command word 'describe' in a question, you're being asked to show lower-order thinking skills like knowledge and understanding. The question will either be worth fewer marks, or you will need to make more points if it is worth more marks.

The command word 'explain' is asking you to show higher-order thinking skills. When you see the command word 'explain', you need to be able to say how or why something happens.

You need to understand all of the relevant command words for the subjects you are taking. Ask your teacher where to find them if you are not sure. It's best not to try to memorise the list of command words, but to become familiar with what command words are asking for by doing lots of practice questions and marking your own work.

How to work with command words

When you first see an exam question, read it through once. Then, read it through again and identify the command word(s). Underline the command word(s) to make it clear to yourself which they are every time you refer back to the question.

You may also want to identify the **content** words in the question and underline them with a different colour. Content words tell you which area of knowledge you need to draw on to answer the question.

In this example, command words are shown in red and underlined with content words in **blue and bold**:

1   a   Explain **four** reasons why **governments** might **support business start-ups**.   [8]

Adapted from Cambridge IGCSE Business Studies (0450) Q1a Paper 21 June 2022

Marking your own work using the mark scheme will help you get even better at understanding command words and knowing how to give good answers for each.

Work with mark scheme awareness

The most transformative thing that any student can do to improve their marks is to work with mark schemes. This means using mark schemes to mark your own work at every opportunity.

Many students are very nervous about marking their own work as they do not feel experienced or qualified enough. However, being brave enough to try to mark your own work and taking the time to get good at it will improve your marks hugely.

Why marking your own work makes such a big difference

Marking your own work can help you to improve your answers in the following ways:

1   Answering the question

Having a deep and detailed understanding of what is required by the question enables you to answer the question more clearly and more accurately.

It can also help you to give the required information using fewer words and in less time, as you can avoid including unrelated points or topics in your answer.

2   Using subject-specific vocabulary

Every subject has subject-specific vocabulary. This includes technical terms for objects or concepts in a subject, such as mitosis and meiosis in biology. It also includes how you talk about the subject, using appropriate vocabulary that may differ from everyday language. For example, in any science subject you might be asked to describe the trend on a graph.

Your answer could say it 'goes up fast' or your answer could say it 'increases rapidly'. You would not get marks for saying 'it goes up fast', but you would for saying it 'increases rapidly'. This is the difference between everyday language and formal, scientific language.

When you answer lots of practice questions, you become fluent in the language specific to your subject.

3 Knowing how much to write

It's very common for students to either write too much or too little to answer questions. Becoming familiar with the mark schemes for many different questions will help you to gain a better understanding of how much you need to write in order to get a good mark.

4 Structuring your answer

There are often clues in questions about how to structure your answer. However, mark schemes give you an even stronger idea of the structure you should use in your answers.

For example, if a question says:

'Describe and explain two reasons why…'

You can give a clear answer by:

- describing reason 1

- explaining reason 1

- describing reason 2

- explaining reason 2.

Having a very clear structure will also make it easier to identify where you have earned marks. This means that you're more likely to be awarded the number of marks you deserve.

5 Keeping to time

Answering the question, using subject-specific vocabulary, knowing how much to write and giving a clear structure to your answer will all help you to keep to time in an exam. You will not waste time by writing too much for any answer. Therefore, you will have sufficient time to give a good answer to every question.

How to answer exam questions brilliantly

Understand connections between concepts

One of the higher-level thinking skills in Bloom's Taxonomy is **synthesis**. Synthesis means making connections between different areas of knowledge. You may have heard about synoptic links. Making synoptic links is the same as showing the thinking skill of synthesis.

Exam questions that ask you to show your synthesis skills are usually worth the highest number of marks on an exam paper. To write good answers to these questions, you need to spend time thinking about the links between the topics you've studied before you arrive in your exam. A great way of doing this is using mind maps.

How to create a mind map

To create a mind map:

1 Use a large piece of paper and several different coloured pens.

2   Write the name of your subject in the middle. Then, write the key topic areas evenly spaced around the edge, each with a different colour.

3   Then, around each topic area, start to write the detail of what you can remember. If you find something that is connected with something you studied in another topic, you can draw a line linking the two things together.

This is a good way of practising your retrieval of information as well as linking topics together.

Answering synoptic exam questions

You will recognise questions that require you to make links between concepts because they have a higher number of marks. You will have practised them using this book and the accompanying resources.

To answer a synoptic exam question:

1   **Identify the command and content words**. You are more likely to find command words like **discuss** and **explain** in these questions. They might also have phrases like 'the connection between'.

2   **Make a plan for your answer**. It is worth taking a short amount of time to think about what you're going to write in your answer. Think carefully about what information you're going to put in, the links between the different pieces of information and how you're going to structure your answer to make your ideas clear.

3   **Use linking words and phrases in your answer**. For example, 'therefore', 'because', 'due to', 'since' or 'this means that'.

Here is an example of an English Literature exam question that requires you to make synoptic links in your answer.

1   Discuss **Carol Ann Duffy's exploration of childhood** in her poetry.

    Refer to **two** poems in your answer.   [25]

Content words are shown in blue; command words are shown in red.

This question is asking you to explore the theme of childhood in Duffy's poetry. You need to choose two of her poems to refer to in your answer. This means you need a good knowledge of her poetry, and to be familiar with her exploration of childhood, so that you can easily select two poems that will give you plenty to say in your answer.

Keep to time

Managing your time in exams is really important. Some students do not achieve to the best of their abilities because they run out of time to answer all the questions. However, if you manage your time well, you will be able to attempt every question on the exam paper.

Why is it important to attempt all the questions on an exam paper?

If you attempt every question on a paper, you have the best chance of achieving the highest mark you are capable of.

Students who manage their time poorly in exams will often spend far too long on some questions and not even attempt others. Most students are unlikely to get full marks on many questions, but you will get zero marks for the questions you don't answer. You can maximise your marks by giving an answer to every question.

Minutes per mark

The most important way to keep to time is knowing how many minutes you can spend on each mark.

For example, if your exam paper has 90 marks available and you have 90 minutes, you know there is 1 mark per minute.

Therefore, if you have a five-mark question, you should spend five minutes on it.

Sometimes, you can give a good answer in less time than you have budgeted using the minutes per mark technique. If this happens, you will have more time to spend on questions that use higher-order thinking skills, or more time on checking your work.

How to get faster at answering exam questions

The best way to get faster at answering exam questions is to do lots of practice. You should practise each question type that will be in your exam, marking your own work, so that you know precisely how that question works and what is required by the question. Use the questions in this book to get better and better at answering each question type.

Use the 'Slow, Slow, Quick' technique to get faster.

Take your time answering questions when you first start practising them. You may answer them with the support of the textbook, your notes or the mark scheme. These things will support you with your content knowledge, the language you use in your answer and the structure of your answer.

Every time you practise this question type, you will get more confident and faster. You will become experienced with this question type, so that it is easy for you to recall the subject knowledge and write it down using the correct language and a good structure.

Calculating marks per minute

Use this calculation to work out how long you have for each mark:

Total time in the exam / Number of marks available = Minutes per mark

Calculate how long you have for a question worth more than one mark like this:

Minutes per mark × Marks available for this question
= Number of minutes for this question

What about time to check your work?

It is a very good idea to check your work at the end of an exam. You need to work out if this is feasible with the minutes per mark available to you. If you're always rushing to finish the questions, you shouldn't budget checking time. However, if you usually have time to spare, then you can budget checking time.

To include checking time in your minutes per mark calculation:

(Total time in the exam – Checking time) / Number of marks available
= Minutes per mark

Know what a good answer looks like

It is much easier to give a good answer if you know what a good answer looks like.

Use these methods to know what a good answer looks like.

1 **Sample answers** – you can find sample answers in these places:

   - from your teacher

   - written by your friends or other members of your class

   - in this book.

2 **Look at mark schemes** – mark schemes are full of information about what you should include in your answers. Get familiar with mark schemes to gain a better understanding of the type of things a good answer would contain.

3 **Feedback from your teacher** – if you are finding it difficult to improve your exam skills for a particular type of question, ask your teacher for detailed feedback. You should also look at their comments on your work in detail.

Give yourself the best chance of success

Reflection on progress

As you prepare for your exam, it's important to reflect on your progress. Taking time to think about what you're doing well and what could be improved brings more focus to your revision. Reflecting on progress also helps you to continuously improve your knowledge and exam skills.

How do you reflect on progress?

Use the 'reflection' feature in this book to help you reflect on your progress during your exam preparation. Then, at the end of each revision session, take a few minutes to think about the following:

	What went well? What would you do the same next time?	What didn't go well? What would you do differently next time?
Your subject knowledge		
How you revised your subject knowledge – did you use active retrieval techniques?		
Your use of subject-specific and academic language		
Understanding the question by identifying command words and content words		
Giving a clear structure to your answer		
Keeping to time		
Marking your own work		

Remember to check for silly mistakes – things like missing the units out after you carefully calculated your answer.

Use the mark scheme to mark your own work. Every time you mark your own work, you will be recognising the good and bad aspects of your work, so that you can progressively give better answers over time.

When do you need to come back to this topic or skill?

Earlier in this section of the book, we talked about revision skills and the importance of spaced retrieval. When you reflect on your progress, you need to think about how soon you need to return to the topic or skill you've just been focusing on.

For example, if you were really disappointed with your subject knowledge, it would be a good idea to do some more active retrieval and practice questions on this topic tomorrow. However, if you did really well you can feel confident you know this topic and come back to it again in three weeks' or a month's time.

The same goes for exam skills. If you were disappointed with how you answered the question, you should look at some sample answers and try this type of question again soon. However, if you did well, you can move on to other types of exam questions.

Improving your memory of subject knowledge

Sometimes students slip back into using passive revision techniques, such as only reading the Coursebook or their notes, rather than also using active revision techniques, like testing themselves using flip cards or blurting.

You can avoid this mistake by observing how well your learning is working as you revise. You should be thinking to yourself, 'Am I remembering this? Am I understanding this? Is this revision working?'

If the answer to any of those questions is 'no', then you need to change what you're doing to revise this particular topic. For example, if you don't understand, you could look up your topic in a different textbook in the school library to see if a different explanation helps. Or you could see if you can find a video online that brings the idea to life.

You are in control

When you're studying for exams it's easy to think that your teachers are in charge. However, you have to remember that you are studying for your exams and the results you get will be yours and no one else's.

That means you have to take responsibility for all your exam preparation. You have the power to change how you're preparing if what you're doing isn't working. You also have control over what you revise and when: you can make sure you focus on your weaker topics and skills to improve your achievement in the subject.

This isn't always easy to do. Sometimes you have to find an inner ability that you have not used before. But, if you are determined enough to do well, you can find what it takes to focus, improve and keep going.

What is test anxiety?

Do you get worried or anxious about exams? Does your worry or anxiety impact how well you do in tests and exams?

Test anxiety is part of your natural stress response.

The stress response evolved in animals and humans many thousands of years ago to help keep them alive. Let's look at an example.

The stress response in the wild

Imagine an impala grazing in the grasslands of east Africa. It's happily and calmly eating grass in its herd in what we would call the parasympathetic state of rest and repair.

Then the impala sees a lion. The impala suddenly panics because its life is in danger. This state of panic is also known as the stressed or sympathetic state. The sympathetic state presents itself in three forms: flight, fight and freeze.

The impala starts to run away from the lion. Running away is known as the flight stress response.

The impala might not be fast enough to run away from the lion. The lion catches it but has a loose grip. The impala struggles to try to get away. This struggle is the fight stress response.

However, the lion gets an even stronger grip on the impala. Now the only chance of the impala surviving is playing dead. The impala goes limp, its heart rate and breathing slows. This is called the freeze stress response. The lion believes that it has killed the impala so it drops the impala to the ground. Now the impala can switch back into the flight response and run away.

The impala is now safe – the different stages of the stress response have saved its life.

What has the impala got to do with your exams?

When you feel test anxiety, you have the same physiological stress responses as an impala being hunted by a lion. Unfortunately, the human nervous system cannot tell the difference between a life-threatening situation, such as being chased by a lion, and the stress of taking an exam.

If you understand how the stress response works in the human nervous system, you will be able to learn techniques to reduce test anxiety.

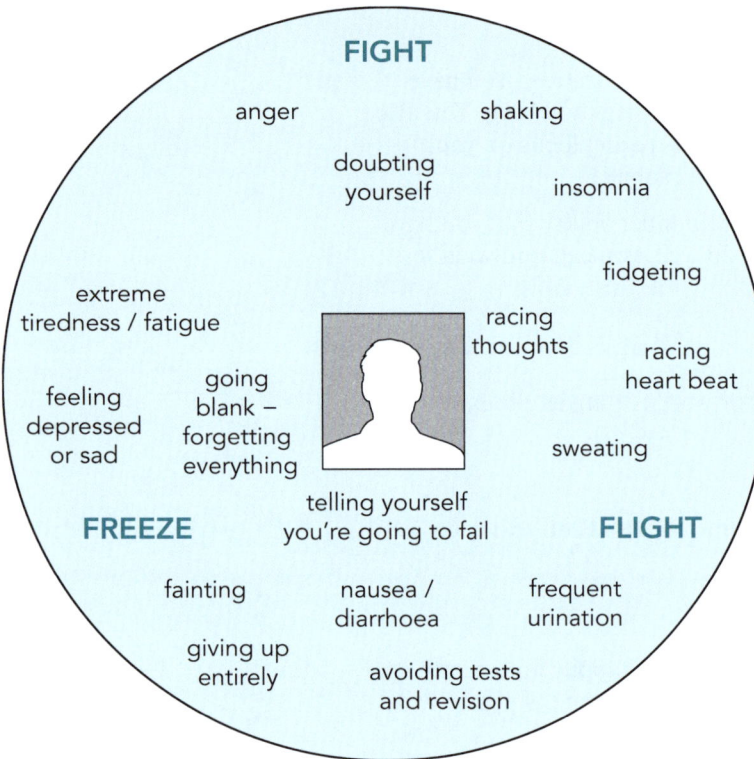

The role of the vagus nerve in test anxiety

The vagus nerve is the part of your nervous system that determines your stress response. Vagus means 'wandering' in Latin, so the vagus nerve is also known as the 'wandering nerve'. The vagus nerve wanders from your brain, down each side of your body, to nearly all your organs, including your lungs, heart, kidneys, liver, digestive system and bladder.

If you are in a stressful situation, like an exam, your vagus nerve sends a message to all these different organs to activate their stress response. Here are some common examples:

- **Heart** beats faster.

- **Kidneys** produce more adrenaline so that you can run, making you fidgety and distracted.

- **Digestive system** and **bladder** want to eliminate all waste products so that energy can be used for fight or flight.

If you want to feel calmer about your revision and exams, you need to do two things to help you move into the parasympathetic, or rest and repair, state:

1   Work with your vagus nerve to send messages of safety through your body.
2   Change your perception of the test so that you see it as safe and not dangerous.

How to cope with test anxiety

1   Be well prepared

Good preparation is the most important part of managing test anxiety. The better your preparation, the more confident you will be. If you are confident, you will not perceive the test or exam as dangerous, so the sympathetic nervous system responses of fight, flight and freeze are less likely to happen.

This book is all about helping you to be well prepared and building your confidence in your knowledge and ability to answer exam questions well. Working through the knowledge recall questions will help you to become more confident in your knowledge of the subject. The practice questions and exam skills questions will help you to become more confident in communicating your knowledge in an exam.

To be well prepared, look at the advice in the rest of this chapter and use it as you work through the questions in this book.

2   Work with your vagus nerve

The easiest way to work with your vagus nerve to tell it that you're in a safe situation is through your breathing. This means breathing deeply into the bottom of your lungs, so that your stomach expands, and then breathing out for longer than you breathed in. You can do this with counting.

Breathe in deeply, expanding your abdomen, for the count of four; breathe out drawing your navel back towards your spine for the count of five, six or seven. Repeat this at least three times. However, you can do it for as long as it takes for you to feel calm.

The important thing is that you breathe out for longer than you breathe in. This is because when you breathe in, your heart rate increases slightly, and when you breathe out, your heart rate decreases slightly. If you're spending more time breathing out overall, you will be decreasing your heart rate over time.

3   Feel it

Anxiety is an uncomfortable, difficult thing to feel. That means that many people try to run away from anxious feelings. However, this means the stress just gets stored in your body for you to feel later.

When you feel anxious, follow these four steps:

1   Pause.
2   Place one hand on your heart and one hand on your stomach.
3   Notice what you're feeling.
4   Stay with your feelings.

What you will find is that if you are willing to experience what you feel for a minute or two, the feeling of anxiety will usually pass very quickly.

4   Write or talk it out

If your thoughts are moving very quickly, it is often better to get them out of your mind and on to paper.

You could take a few minutes to write down everything that comes through your mind, then rip up your paper and throw it away. If you don't like writing, you can speak aloud alone or to someone you trust.

Other ways to break the stress cycle

Exercise and movement	Being friendly	Laughter
• Run or walk. • Dance. • Lift weights. • Practise yoga. Anything that involves moving your body is helpful.	• Chat to someone in your study break. • Talk to the cashier when you buy your lunch.	• Watch or listen to a funny show on TV or online. • Talk with someone who makes you laugh. • Look at photos of fun times.
Have a hug	**Releasing emotions**	**Creativity**
• Hug a friend or relative. • Cuddle a pet, e.g. a cat. Hug for 20 seconds or until you feel calm and relaxed.	It is healthy to release negative or sad emotions. Crying is often a quick way to get rid of these difficult feelings so if you feel like you need to cry, allow it.	• Paint, draw or sketch. • Sew, knit or crochet. • Cook or build something.

If you have long-term symptoms of anxiety, it is important to tell someone you trust and ask for help.

Your perfect revision session

1 Intention

What do you want to achieve in this revision session?
- Choose an area of knowledge or an exam skill that you want to focus on.
- Choose some questions from this book that focus on this knowledge area or skill.
- Gather any other resources you will need, e.g. pen, paper, flashcards, Coursebook.

2 Focus

Set your focus for the session
- Remove distractions from your study area, e.g. leave your phone in another room.
- Write down on a piece of paper or sticky note the knowledge area or skill you're intending to focus on.
- Close your eyes and take three deep breaths, with the exhale longer than the inhale.

3 Revision

Revise your knowledge and understanding
- To improve your knowledge and understanding of the topic, use your Coursebook, notes or flashcards, including active learning techniques.
- To improve your exam skills, look at previous answers, teacher feedback, mark schemes, sample answers or examiners' reports.

4 Practice

Answer practice questions
- Use the questions in this book, or in the additional online resources, to practise your exam skills.
- If the exam is soon, do this in timed conditions without the support of the Coursebook or your notes.
- If the exam is a long time away, you can use your notes and resources to help you.

5 Feedback

Mark your answers
- Use mark schemes to mark your work.
- Reflect on what you've done well and what you could do to improve next time.

6 Next steps

What have you learned about your progress from this revision session? What do you need to do next?
- What did you do well? Feel good about these things, and know it's safe to set these things aside for a while.
- What do you need to work on? How are you going to improve? Make a plan to get better at the things you didn't do well or didn't know.

7 Rest

Take a break
- Do something completely different to rest: get up, move or do something creative or practical.
- Remember that rest is an important part of studying, as it gives your brain a chance to integrate your learning.

Physical Geography

1 Rivers

KNOWLEDGE FOCUS

You will answer questions on:

- 1.1 The main hydrological characteristics and processes which operate in rivers and drainage basins

- 1.2 The main landforms associated with these processes

- 1.3 Rivers present opportunities and hazards for people

EXAM SKILLS FOCUS

In this topic you will:

- show that you understand what command words are

- show that you understand the command word 'explain' and answer an 'explain' question

- show that you understand the command word 'compare' and answer a 'compare' question.

Command words form the foundation for any assessment question. They are not specific to geography. Instead, they are instructions, such as 'explain' or 'compare'. While command words do not specify which topics to write about, they do guide you on how to approach a particular question. Each topic of this book will contain questions using at least two different command words, to allow you to practise.

The command word 'explain' means to set out purposes or reasons / make the relationships between things clear / say why and/or how and support with relevant evidence. This means you should say why or how something happens. 'Explain' questions assess your understanding of geographical systems, theories and processes. This type of question is common in geography exams and can feature in all three papers.

The command word 'compare' means to identify/comment on similarities and/or differences. Comparison questions require you to focus on two or more different features or concepts, recognising what they have in common and how they differ from one another. Key words such as 'both', 'however', 'similarly' and 'in contrast' are useful for these types of questions.

1.1 The main hydrological characteristics and processes which operate in rivers and drainage basins

It is crucial to understand what each command word means, so you know what a question is asking you to do. Look at the questions below to see the difference between 'describe' and 'explain' questions. While these questions appear similar at first, the command words demand entirely different responses. Recognising this distinction is an essential skill to develop, so you can focus your answer correctly.

1   Describe how the velocity of a river changes as it flows downhill.   [2]

2   Explain why the velocity of a river changes as it flows downhill.   [4]

You will have the opportunity to practise more questions with different command words in each topic of this book.

> ### REFLECTION
>
> Do you understand the difference between 'describe' and 'explain' questions? Seeing them side by side, as with Questions 1 and 2, makes you consider the difference between the two. In this example, 'describe' means say **how** the velocity changes, and 'explain' means say **why** the velocity changes. Creating your own 'describe' and 'explain' questions can help you to recognise the difference.

3   Figure 1.1 shows the water cycle, or hydrological cycle. Identify the key terms that correctly complete Boxes A, B and C.

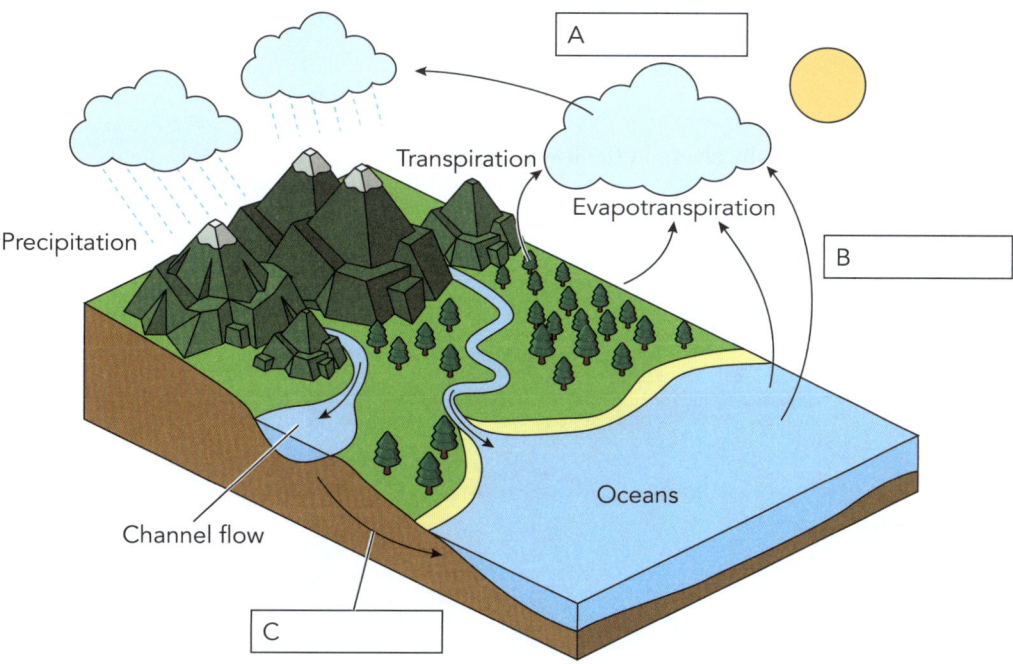

Figure 1.1: The water cycle

4   Copy the following text and complete the gaps using the words below from Topic 1.

watershed   **tributary**   **upland**   **confluence**

A drainage basin is an area of land drained by a river and its tributaries. It moves water from _____ areas towards the sea. The _____ is the boundary between each drainage basin. A _____is the meeting point between two rivers of similar size, and a _____ is a smaller river or stream that feeds into the main river channel.

5   There are three main river processes: erosion, transportation and deposition. Sort the key terms from Table 1.1 into two categories: erosion processes and transportation processes.

| traction |
| hydraulic action |
| saltation |
| abrasion |
| attrition |
| suspension |

Table 1.1: River processes

UNDERSTAND THESE TERMS

- Abrasion
- Attrition
- Drainage basin
- Hydraulic action
- Saltation
- Suspension
- Traction
- Wetted perimeter

6   Which processes of erosion and transportation are missing from Table 1.1?

Questions with the command word 'explain' require you to show that you understand how or why something occurs. These questions test your ability to connect ideas and apply your knowledge effectively. See if you can answer these 'explain' questions.

7   Explain how erosion, transportation and deposition work together in a river.   [4]

8   Explain why vertical erosion is more likely to take place in the upper course of a river.   [4]

9   Figure 1.2 shows a lowland river. Explain why rivers in the lower course have a larger wetted perimeter.   [2]

Figure 1.2: A lowland river

10 Explain why alluvium (deposited material) is often found in the middle and lower courses of a river. [4]

1.2 The main landforms associated with these processes

« RECALL AND CONNECT 1 «

River processes and landforms are very similar to coastal processes and landforms. See if you can answer the following questions, linked to Topic 2, 'Coastal environments'.

a Name two coastal landforms of erosion.

b Explain how concordant coastlines differ from discordant coastlines.

1 Explain how waterfalls are formed, using labelled diagrams to support your answer.

2 Which of the following landforms are found in the upper course of a river?

- waterfall
- rapids
- oxbow lake
- delta
- floodplain
- gorge

3 How do levees form?

For questions that use the command word 'compare', you should identify or comment on similarities and/or differences. Carefully read the question to understand what two or more things you are being asked to compare. 'Compare' questions are commonly shorter response questions. You should look at the number of marks available to help you to decide roughly how much to write.

4 Compare the features of rapids and waterfalls. [3]

5 Figure 1.3 shows a cross-section of a river meander. Compare the outside of the meander (A) with the inside of the meander (B). [3]

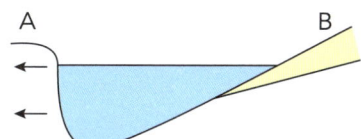

Figure 1.3: A cross-section through a meander bend in a river

6   Figures 1.4 and 1.5 show two sections of the River Dove as it flows through Derbyshire and Staffordshire in the UK. Compare the characteristics of the river and its valley in the two locations.   [3]

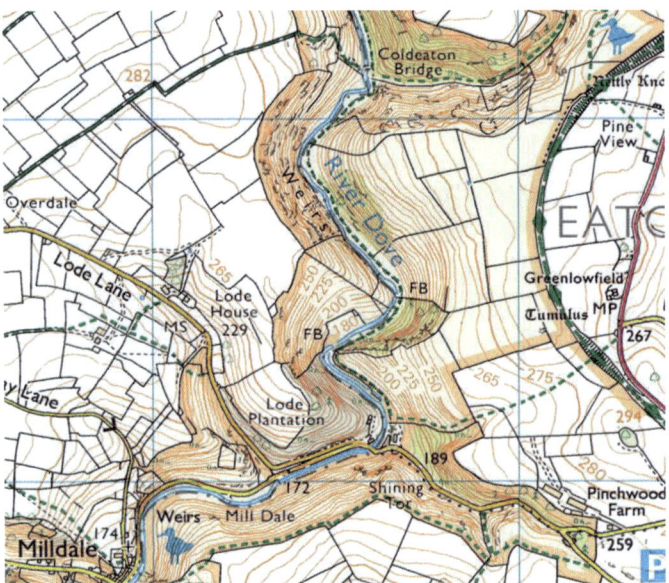

Figure 1.4: The River Dove at Milldale, Derbyshire

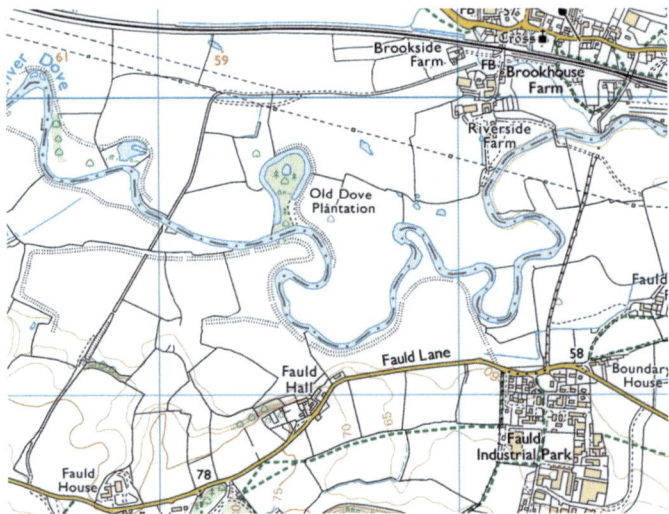

Figure 1.5: The River Dove at Fauld, Staffordshire

1.3 Rivers present opportunities and hazards for people

1   List three opportunities that rivers can provide.

2   How can agriculture contribute to river pollution?

3   Name one human cause of flooding and one natural cause of flooding.

Attempt the questions below to practise answering both 'explain' and 'compare' questions. Remember that each command word requires a different approach. Consider the command word carefully when answering, rather than focusing solely on the topic content.

4   Compare the impacts on people of river flooding and pollution.   [6]

5   Explain the economic impacts of flooding.   [4]

6   Compare the effectiveness of hard engineering and soft engineering techniques used in the management of flooding.   [6]

7   Explain how afforestation can help to prevent river flooding.   [3]

REFLECTION

How well do you know your detailed specific examples? Do you struggle to remember facts about different places? Sometimes it helps to annotate maps of places to show where different events have taken place. For example, you can annotate a map of a river to show where the human and natural causes of flooding originated. Seeing this information on a map can sometimes help you to understand places that you may not have visited before. Does this technique help you to understand detailed specific examples?

≪ RECALL AND CONNECT 2 ≪

Rivers can be a useful resource. They are frequently used in the generation of energy. See if you can answer this question about rivers as a resource, linked to Topic 10, 'Resource provision'.

a   How does hydroelectric power (HEP) use rivers to generate electricity?

b   Is HEP a renewable or non-renewable source of energy? Explain your answer.

SELF-ASSESSMENT CHECKLIST

Let's revisit the knowledge focus and exam skills focus for this topic.
Decide how confident you are with each statement.

Now I can	Show it	Needs more work	Almost there	Confident to move on
Explain the features and processes of drainage basins	Define watershed, confluence, tributary, source and mouth.			
Explain the different river processes	How are the processes of erosion, transportation and deposition connected in a river system?			
Describe the landforms that are found in different stages of a river and explain how they are formed	List two landforms found in the upper, middle and lower courses of a river.			
Understand the hazards and opportunities that rivers provide	With reference to rivers, give two examples of hazards and two examples of opportunities.			
Understand the command word 'explain'	Answer an 'explain' question confidently, such as 'Explain how waterfalls form.'			
Understand the command word 'compare'	Answer a 'compare' question confidently, such as 'Compare the upper and lower courses of a river.'			
Understand what command words are	Describe the difference between an 'explain' question and a 'compare' question.			

2 Coastal environments

KNOWLEDGE FOCUS

You will answer questions on:

- 2.1 Physical processes that shape the coast
- 2.2 The main landforms associated with these processes
- 2.3 Coasts present opportunities and hazards for people

EXAM SKILLS FOCUS

In this topic you will:

- show that you understand the command word 'describe' and answer a 'describe' question
- recognise that you need to keep to time in your exam.

The command word 'describe' means to state the points of a topic / give characteristics and main features. You do not need to give reasons in an answer to a 'describe' question. You only need to focus on the points of a topic or the characteristics and main features of what you have been asked to describe.

Keeping to time is important in your exam. If you understand how much time to spend on a particular question, then you can focus your answer and know when to move on to the next question. This will help you to avoid spending too long on one question which could result in you running out of time in the exam. As a very rough guide, you should aim to spend between 1–1.5 minutes per mark. For some questions, you may need longer for reading time and planning, and for other questions, you may be able to answer the question very quickly.

2.1 Physical processes that shape the coast

Understanding the types of processes that shape the coast is important. Test your knowledge on the physical processes that shape the coast using the questions below. There is some overlap with river processes so make sure that you are referring to the appropriate environment in your responses.

1   Sort the following terms into 'erosion processes' or 'deposition processes'.

   • hydraulic action

   • longshore drift

   • corrasion

   • a wave losing energy and dropping material on a beach

   • formation of a spit

   • corrosion

2   Decide if the following statements are true or false:

   a   Swash carries sediment down the beach.

   b   Longshore drift is influenced by the direction of prevailing winds.

   c   Suspension involves large pebbles rolling along the seabed.

3   How does wave refraction help to form headlands and bays?

4   Produce a labelled diagram of a destructive wave, showing its main characteristics.

'Describe' questions require you to give the main characteristics of something. For example, when describing how sediment moves down the coast, you need to state **how** this occurs. You do not need to explain **why**. When describing a figure, you need to 'say what you see'. Only use the resource. There is also no need to give reasons for the trends or patterns that you can see, as that would be explaining.

5   Describe how sediment is moved along the coast.   [5]

6   Study Figure 2.1. Describe the impacts of installing groynes on this coastline shown in Figure 2.1.   [5]

UNDERSTAND THESE TERMS
• Hydraulic action
• Corrasion
• Corrosion
• Swash
• Spit
• Suspension
• Wave refraction
• Longshore drift
• Destructive wave
• Headland
• Bay

Figure 2.1: A beach with wooden groynes   [2]

2.2 The main landforms associated with these processes

≪ RECALL AND CONNECT 1 ≪

Coasts can provide tidal, solar and wind energy to meet our growing energy needs. Many coastal areas also contain major seaports where food is transported all around the world. Answer the questions below to test your understanding of Topic 10, 'Resource provision'.

a What are the benefits of renewable energy?

b What are the drawbacks of renewable energy?

c Name three inputs used on a farm.

d What are some strategies that improve food supply?

UNDERSTAND THESE TERMS

- Cliff
- Wave-cut platform
- Cave
- Arch
- Stack
- Stump

---

1 Match the landform, a-d, with its description, 1–4.

a	headland	1	A vertical column of rock that stands alone in the sea, detached from the mainland.
b	bay	2	A natural opening in a rock face where the sea has eroded through a headland.
c	stack	3	A curved indentation of the coastline between two headlands.
d	arch	4	A narrow piece of land that sticks out from the coastline into the sea.

2 Complete the gaps in these sentences about coastal landforms using the words below.

dunes   wave-cut platform   direction   constructive waves

hook   cave   marsh   cliff   stack   hook   beach

vegetation   bar

a As a result of wave action at the base of a _____ , a wave-cut notch can develop over time between the points at which low tide and high tide reach. As the cliff erodes, collapses and retreats over time, a _____ is left behind.

b A typical sequence for coastal erosional landforms is: crack, _____ , arch, _____ , stump.

c A _____ is a common landform of deposition and occurs in a sheltered area, such as a bay, where waves deposit sand or pebbles. _____ help build up a beach, as they have a greater swash than backwash.

d   Coastal _____ are formed from loose sand that winds blow onshore. Debris on the beach slows the wind down, causing the wind to deposit the sand. Over time these sand mounds grow into larger dunes, as more sand is deposited and _____ stabilises them.

e   A spit forms where there is a change in _____ of the coastline, such as at a headland. If the spit continues to grow and is influenced by changes in wave patterns or wind direction, it may curve at its outer end. This forms a _____ . Often a _____ develops behind a spit. If a spit continues to grow across a bay and connects two headlands together, it forms a coastal _____ .

3   What landforms may be formed along a discordant coastline and why?

4   Describe a concordant coastline.   [3]

5   Study Figure 2.2. Describe the landform labelled X in Figure 2.2.   [5]

UNDERSTAND THESE TERMS
• Beach
• Sand dune
• Bar
• Concordant coastline
• Discordant coastline

X

Figure 2.2: A coastal landform

REFLECTION

After reading a 'describe' question, how do you know what the key features or components are that you need to focus on? Do you have any strategies that help you focus on what the question is asking you to do? Now look back at some of your previous answers to 'describe' questions. What made them good?

2.3 Coasts present opportunities and hazards for people

« RECALL AND CONNECT 2 «

Hazardous environments like coasts can provide both opportunities and hazards for people. Answer the questions below to test your understanding of Topic 4, 'Tectonic hazards', which represents another hazardous environment.

a What are the economic benefits of living near a volcano?

b Name three scales that are used to measure earthquakes.

c What is a lahar?

d Draw a labelled diagram to show the main features of a cinder cone volcano.

1 Copy and complete Tables 2.1 and 2.2.

Hard engineering technique	Description	Advantage	Disadvantage	Level of sustainability
Sea wall				
Groynes				

Table 2.1: Hard engineering techniques

Soft engineering technique	Description	Advantage	Disadvantage	Level of sustainability
Beach nourishment				
Managed retreat				

Table 2.2: Soft engineering techniques

2 Decide if the following statements are true or false.

a Rising sea levels can lead to increased flooding in coastal areas.

b Tourism always has a negative impact on coastal environments.

c Coastal defences can help reduce the risk of erosion and flooding.

d Living near the coast offers no economic benefits.

3 What is coral bleaching?

4 What are some threats to mangroves?

Keeping to time is really important in your exam. If you do not manage your time properly, you may miss out questions. If you don't give an answer to a question, you won't get any marks for that question. Before you answer a question, work out how long you should spend on it – remember that you should aim to spend between 1–1.5 minutes per mark.

Decide how long you should spend answering the following questions, and then time yourself answering the questions.

5 Describe **three** impacts of a tropical storm. [3]

6 Study Figure 2.3. Describe the distribution of coral reefs. [3]

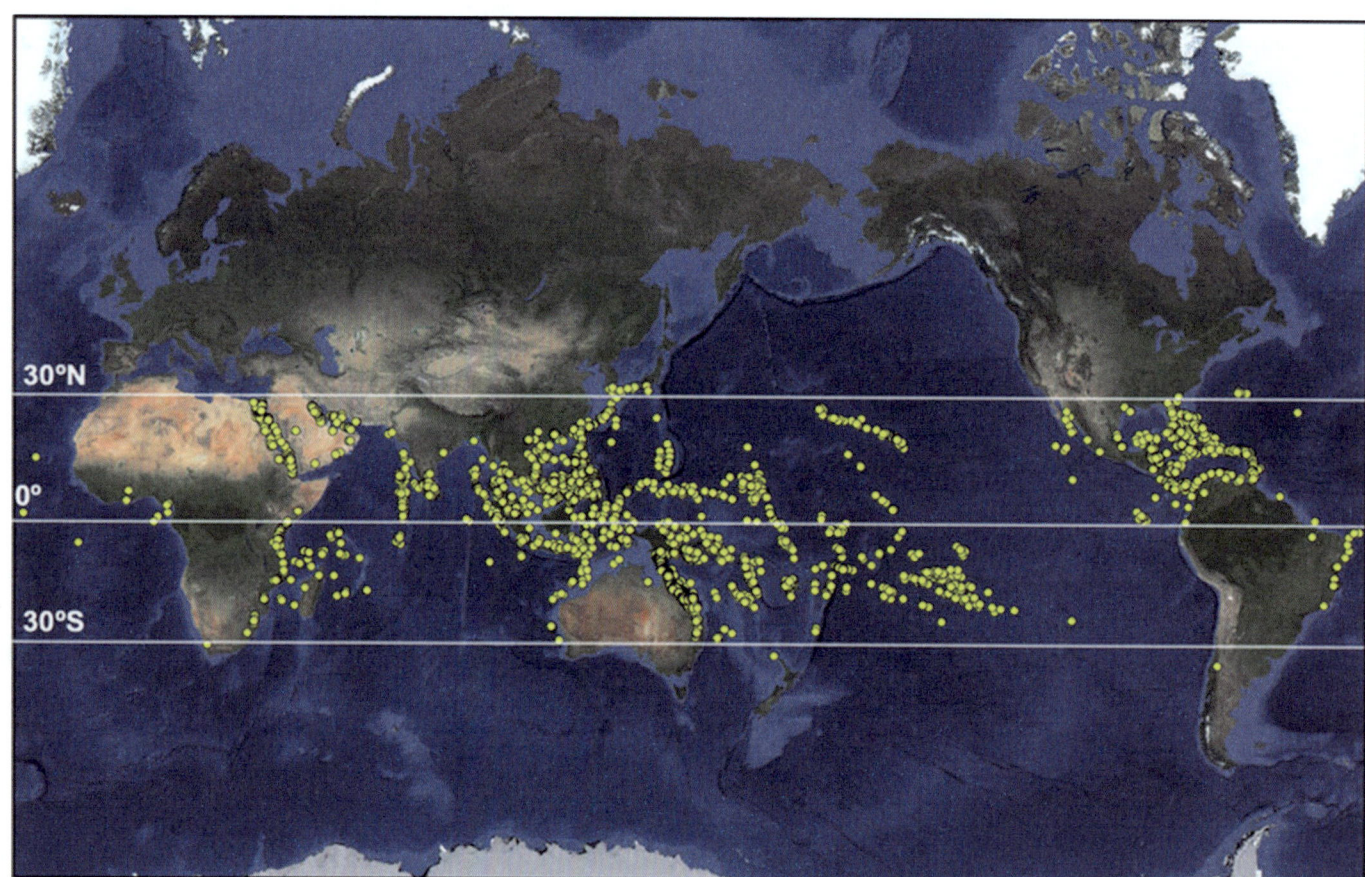

Figure 2.3: The global distribution of coral reefs

7 Describe **two** opportunities of living near the coast. [4]

8 Using an example you have studied, describe the impacts of a tropical storm. [7]

UNDERSTAND THESE TERMS

- Hard engineering
- Soft engineering
- Coral bleaching

REFLECTION

How did you find answering the questions within a set time? Did you have enough time to answer the questions? Is there anything you can do differently next time to keep your answers on time?

SELF-ASSESSMENT CHECKLIST

Let's revisit the knowledge focus and exam skills focus for this topic.
Decide how confident you are with each statement.

Now I can	Show it	Needs more work	Almost there	Confident to move on
Explain how physical processes shape the coast	Explain how the process of hydraulic action erodes sea cliffs.			
Describe the characteristics and explain the formation of coastal landforms	Explain how the process of longshore drift can lead to the formation of coastal spits.			
Identify opportunities and challenges of living near coasts	Identify three opportunities and three challenges of living near the coast.			
Understand the command word 'describe'	Answer a 'describe' question confidently, such as 'Describe a discordant coastline.'			
Recognise that I need to keep to time in my exam	Answer this question in one minute: 'Give one characteristic of a constructive wave.' [1]			

3 Changing ecosystems

KNOWLEDGE FOCUS

You will answer questions on:

- 3.1 Characteristics of the Antarctic ecosystem
- 3.2 Threats to the Antarctic ecosystem and how they can be managed
- 3.3 Characteristics of the tropical rainforest ecosystem
- 3.4 Threats to tropical rainforest ecosystems and how they can be managed

EXAM SKILLS FOCUS

In this topic you will:

- show that you understand the command word 'sketch' and answer a 'sketch' question
- show that you understand the command word 'discuss' and answer a 'discuss' question
- show that you understand the differences between question types.

The command word 'sketch' requires you to make a simple freehand drawing showing the key features, taking care over proportions. When answering 'sketch' questions, it is important to be clear and accurate, even if the drawing is not highly detailed or very artistic.

The command word 'discuss' means to write about issue(s) or topic(s) in depth in a structured way. When responding to 'discuss' questions, it is important to examine different viewpoints, provide evidence to support your reasoning and reach a reasoned conclusion.

Understanding question types involves identifying the format of the question, such as multiple-choice, short response, long response or gap fill, and knowing what kind of answer each type requires. Recognising the type of question helps you structure your response and ensure that you provide the right amount of detail.

3.1 Characteristics of the Antarctic ecosystem

1   Match the following characteristics, a-d to their definitions, 1–4.

a	flora	**1**	elements of an ecosystem that are living organisms
b	fauna	**2**	plants
c	biotic	**3**	elements of an ecosystem that are non-living or without life
d	abiotic	**4**	animals

2   How have animals adapted to survive in Antarctica?

≪ RECALL AND CONNECT 1 ≪

Glaciers and ice sheets across the world are melting and causing sea-level rise. This is because of climate change. See if you can answer these questions linked to Topic 5, 'Climate change'.

a   What is thermal expansion in relation to climate change?

b   What are ice cores and how have they advanced knowledge about climate change?

UNDERSTAND THESE TERMS

- Ecosystem
- Biotic
- Abiotic
- Thermal expansion

For 'sketch' questions, ensure that your drawing includes key details relevant to the question, even if the drawing is not the most artistic illustration. Start with a light outline and then add labels (short words or phrases that name or identify features of the sketch) and annotations (brief sections of text that describe or explain features and processes in more detail) to explain important features.

3   Sketch a diagram to explain why Antarctica experiences 24 hours of sunlight at certain times of the year.   [5]

4   Sketch a diagram to show why the air above Antarctica is usually cold and dry. [5]

REFLECTION

Sketching can help break down complex information. This means that sketching can make it easier to remember key information. Does sketching make your revision notes easier to understand and remember? Can you include more sketches in your study notes?

3.2 Threats to the Antarctic ecosystem and how they can be managed

1 Copy the Antarctic food chain in Figure 3.1. Then, add the species listed in Table 3.1 to the correct place in Figure 3.1.

Figure 3.1: Flow diagram showing an Antarctic food chain

| Smaller toothed whales |
| Phytoplankton |
| Penguins |
| Krill |

Table 3.1: Antarctic species

2 Under international agreements, which of the following activities are banned in Antarctica?

- collecting scientific data
- military operations
- disposal of nuclear waste
- tourism
- commercial fishing
- mining

3 Use the words below to fill in the gaps about international agreements to protect wildlife in Antarctica.

International Association of Antarctic Tour Operators (IAATO)

Polar Code   **Marine Protected Areas (MPAs)**

International Whaling Commission (IWC)

The _____ imposed a quota system in the 1970s on all parties hunting whales. Two large _____ have been established in the Antarctic to protect biodiversity through protecting those areas from commercial activities. The International Maritime Organization implemented a _____ in 2017 that limits the operation of very large cruise ships in Antarctica. The _____ is working on putting laws in place to manage tourism to the region to limit harm caused by human activity.

When answering 'discuss' questions, it is helpful to structure your answer clearly by dividing it into sections for each viewpoint or argument. Use evidence, such as case studies or data, to support your points and to demonstrate your understanding.

4 Discuss the impact of tourism on Antarctica's ecosystems. [7]

5 Discuss the effectiveness of strategies used to protect Antarctica's ecosystems. [7]

REFLECTION
How did you feel about answering 'discuss' questions? For each question, were you able to show both sides of the argument and come to a conclusion? Can you think of any other 'discuss' questions that link to this topic?

3.3 Characteristics of the tropical rainforest ecosystem

1 Copy and complete Table 3.2 to show the vertical layers of tropical rainforests.

Layer	Approximate height above ground (metres)
	0
	0 to 5
	10 to 20
	30
	Up to 40

Table 3.2: Vertical layers within the tropical rainforest

2 Match the features of rainforest vegetation with the correct image.

epiphytes

lianas

buttress roots

tree ferns

3 What adaptations have plants developed to survive in tropical rainforests?

Use the skills that you've already developed in this topic to attempt the following questions.

4 Sketch a diagram to show why the air above the tropical rainforests is usually hot and wet. [5]

5 Discuss how abiotic factors influence plants and animals in tropical rainforests. [7]

≪ RECALL AND CONNECT 3 ≪

Cacao is a tree that grows in the Amazon Rainforest and other tropical rainforest areas. Cacao is used to make chocolate and other products like cocoa butter. It is a valuable resource that can help a country to develop. See if you can answer these questions linked to Topic 8, 'The challenge of development'.

a   What is Fairtrade?

b   What products are often labelled 'Fairtrade' and how do farmers benefit from Fairtrade?

c   What are the limitations of Fairtrade initiatives in low-income and middle-income countries?

3.4 Threats to tropical rainforest ecosystems and how they can be managed

1   What resources from tropical rainforests do humans use?

2   Use the statements in Table 3.3 to create a flow diagram showing how soil erosion takes place in tropical rainforests.

soil is no longer protected from heavy rain
vegetation is removed
plants are not able to grow
soil erodes, or washes away

Table 3.3: The process of soil erosion

There are a range of question types. Recognising different types of question allows you to tailor your answer accordingly. For example, multiple-choice questions require you to choose the most accurate and relevant answer from a short list. Gap fill questions need you to choose one- or two-word answers from a list to complete a sentence. Some questions have boxes for you to show things like calculations or sketches. Other questions may have diagrams that you need to complete or use to answer a question. Short- and long-response questions are very common; short-response questions require concise and direct answers and are often worth 1–2 marks. Conversely, long-response questions require detailed explanations and are often worth 5–7 marks. There are many opportunities throughout this Topic and others to practise the different types of question.

For questions 3–6, state whether it is a short-response question or long-response question and why. For each question, attempt an answer.

3   State **one** technique that can be used to protect indigenous communities in rainforests.

[1]

4   Compare strategies and techniques for sustainably managing
     tropical rainforests.   [4]

5   Discuss how rainforests can be managed sustainably.   [7]

6   Give **one** strategy to sustainably manage rainforests.   [1]

The digital part of this resource contains multiple-choice questions for each Topic,
so you can practise this question type.

7   What things do you need to consider when answering a multiple-choice question?

REFLECTION

How did you identify which of the above were longer- and shorter-response
questions? Did you look at command words and the number of marks available?
These are both good techniques for determining the length of response to write.

UNDERSTAND THIS TERM

- Sustainable management

SELF-ASSESSMENT CHECKLIST

Let's revisit the knowledge focus and exam skills focus for this topic.
Decide how confident you are with each statement.

Now I can	Show it	Needs more work	Almost there	Confident to move on
Describe the characteristics of the Antarctic ecosystem	Describe the location, climate and features of the Antarctic ecosystem.			
Explain the threats to the Antarctic ecosystem and how these are managed	List three strategies and techniques for managing the Antarctic ecosystem.			
Describe the characteristics of the tropical rainforest ecosystem	Describe the location, climate and features of the tropical rainforest ecosystem.			
Explain the threats to tropical rainforests and how these are managed	List three strategies and techniques for managing the tropical rainforest ecosystem.			
Understand the command word 'sketch'	Answer a sketch question confidently, such as 'Sketch a diagram to show the layers of a tropical rainforest.'			

CONTINUED

Now I can	Show it	Needs more work	Almost there	Confident to move on
Understand the command word 'discuss'	Answer a 'discuss' question confidently, such as 'Discuss the causes and effects of deforestation in tropical rainforests.'			
Understand the differences between question types	List four different types of questions, and how you would approach answering them.			

4 Tectonic hazards

When you answer a question with the command word 'identify', it is asking you to name/select/recognise something. In a question on tectonic hazards, for example, you may be asked to identify the plate boundary where an earthquake has occurred using a tectonic map. Although no explanation is required, your answer must be accurate and directly linked to the data or image provided.

'Suggest' means to apply knowledge and understanding to situations where there are a range of valid responses in order to make proposals/put forward considerations. Unlike questions with fixed answers, 'suggest' questions test your ability to think logically, make predictions and consider different geographical factors. For example, if an earthquake causes widespread destruction in a city, you might suggest that the buildings were poorly constructed and did not have adequate earthquake protection.

4.1 The structure of the Earth and distribution of earthquakes and volcanoes

1 a Label the following in Figure 4.1: crust, mantle, outer core, inner core.

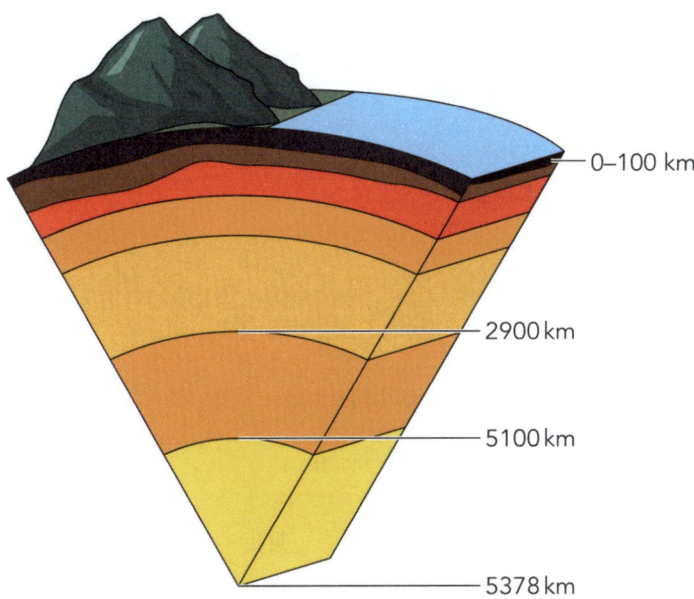

0–100 km

2900 km

5100 km

5378 km

Figure 4.1: The structure of the Earth

b What is meant by the term lithosphere?

c Copy and complete Table 4.1, giving the state of each layer of Earth: 'solid', 'semi-molten' or 'liquid'.

Earth layer	State
crust	
mantle	
outer core	
inner core	

Table 4.1: The states of the layers of the Earth

2 What are the two types of tectonic plates?

3 What is the plate boundary type shown in Figure 4.2?

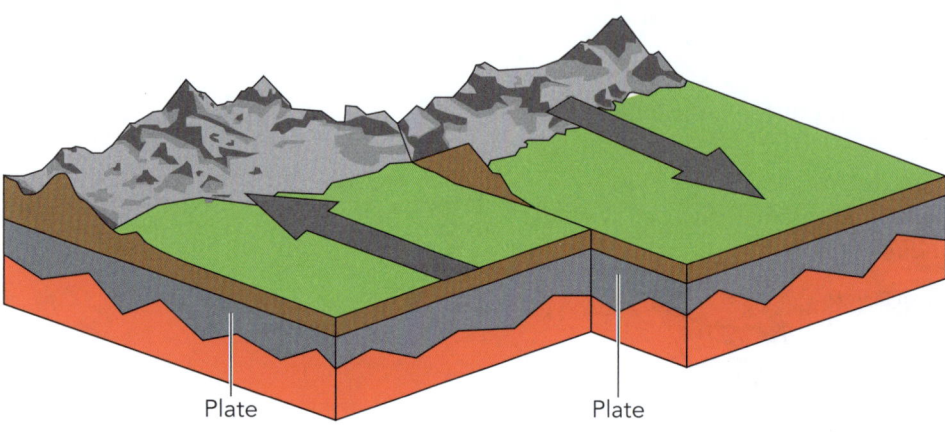

Figure 4.2: A plate boundary

'Identify' questions require you to name/select/recognise something. This could include identifying something from a source. Questions without a source will require you to use your own knowledge, whereas questions that use a source will need you to use it in some way.

4 Identify the plate boundary type shown in Figure 4.3. [1]

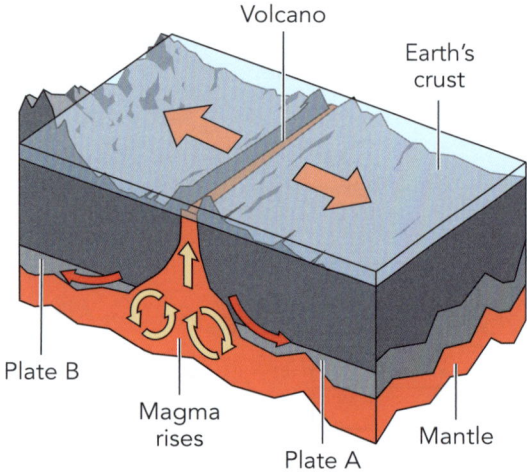

Figure 4.3: A plate boundary

UNDERSTAND THESE TERMS

- Crust
- Mantle
- Lithosphere
- Core
- Magma
- Subduction
- Convergent/ destructive plate boundary
- Transform plate boundary

5 Identify **one** tectonic hazard found at a convergent/destructive plate boundary. [1]

Questions that use the command word 'suggest' require you to apply your knowledge – remember that there is not one fixed answer, so you will have to use logical thinking.

6 Suggest **one** reason an oceanic plate subducts beneath a continental plate. [1]

7 Suggest **one** reason why there are no volcanoes at a transform plate boundary. [1]

REFLECTION

What revision strategies do you find most helpful when revising plate tectonics and plate boundaries? How do you remember which types of tectonic plates are involved? Is there a mnemonic that you can link to this topic to help you? For example, the mnemonic 'transform' can be used to remember what happens at that plate boundary:

T: Two plates slide past each other

R: Rubbing edges create pressure

A: Along fault lines, e.g. the San Andreas Fault

N: No volcanoes

S: Shallow earthquakes

F: Friction builds up between plates

O: Often large earthquakes

R: Releases energy as seismic waves

M: Movement is sideways

≪ RECALL AND CONNECT 1 ≪

Tectonic activity can shape coastal landscapes and influence coastal hazards. Volcanic islands, like those in the Pacific Ocean, are also a result of tectonic processes shaping coastal environments. See if you can answer the questions below from Topic 2, 'Coastal environments'.

a   Add the correct key term into the gaps in the paragraph below. Use the words provided.

corrosion   **attrition**   **hydraulic action**   **corrasion**

Waves erode coastlines through four main processes: _____ , where waves force air into cracks in rocks; _____ , where pebbles and sand grind against cliffs; _____ , where acids in seawater dissolve rock; and _____ , where rock fragments smash against each other, becoming smaller and smoother.

b   Match the coastal feature, a–d to its correct description, 1–4.

	Coastal feature		Description
a	spit	1	A steep rock face formed by erosion at the coast.
b	stack	2	A curved, sandy landform extending into the sea, often with a hooked end.
c	headland	3	A resistant section of rock that juts out into the sea.
d	cliff	4	An isolated pillar of rock left behind after the erosion of an arch.

CAMBRIDGE IGCSE™ AND O LEVEL GEOGRAPHY: EXAM PREPARATION AND PRACTICE

‹‹ RECALL AND CONNECT 1 ‹‹ CONTINUED

c What are two advantages and two disadvantages of hard engineering?

d Name two soft engineering management techniques used along coastlines.

e What are some of the threats to mangroves?

4.2 The processes and features associated with earthquakes and volcanoes

1 a What is the difference between the focus and the epicentre of an earthquake?

b Draw a diagram to show this difference.

2 Draw a labelled diagram to show a cinder cone volcano and its main features.

3 What are the three frequency-of-activity classifications for volcanoes?

4 What are three volcanic hazards?

5 Study Figure 4.4.

UNDERSTAND THESE TERMS
- Focus
- Epicentre

Figure 4.4: A volcano erupting

a Identify the type of volcano shown. [1]

b Suggest **three** hazards associated with this type of volcanic eruption. [3]

6 Study Figure 4.5.

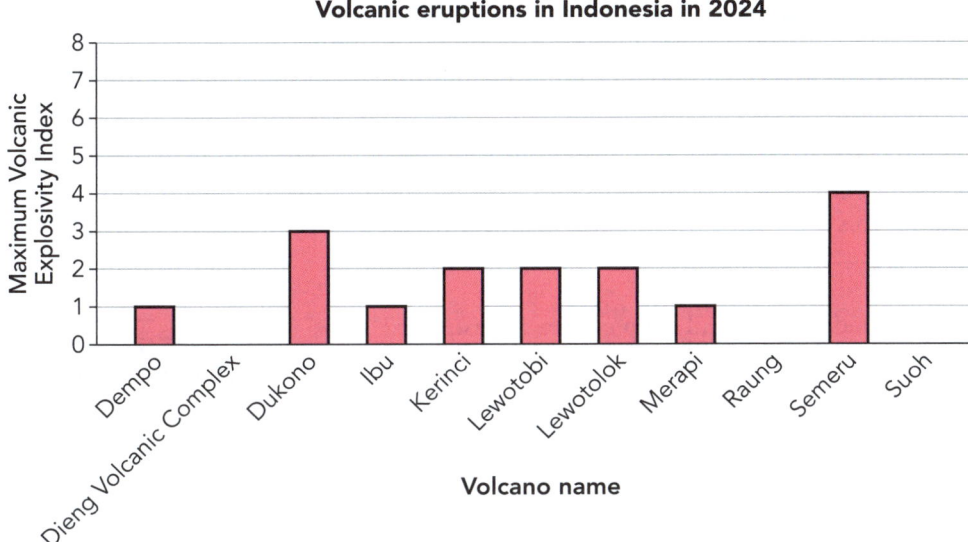

Figure 4.5: Volcanic eruptions in Indonesia in 2024

Identify the volcano with the largest eruption in Indonesia in 2024. [1]

7 Study Figure 4.6.

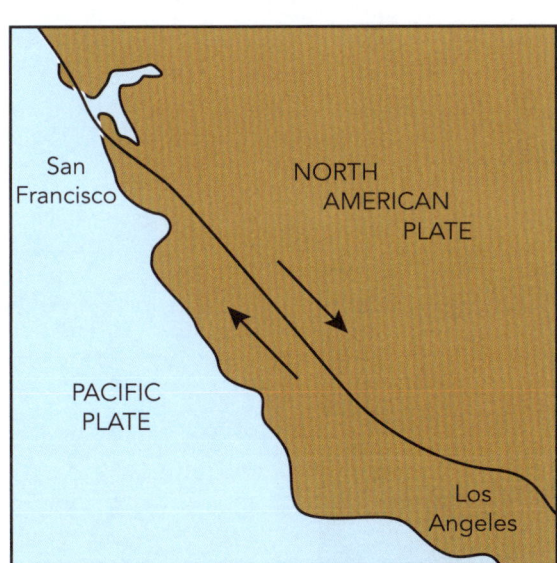

Figure 4.6: A plate boundary in North America

a Identify the plate boundary shown. [1]

b Suggest **one** hazard associated with this plate boundary type. [1]

4.3 The impacts of tectonic hazards

1   What negative impacts are associated with ash fall from a volcanic eruption?

2   What are some positive impacts of volcanic eruptions?

3   What is a lahar?

4   Identify **one** scale used to measure earthquakes. [1]

5   Identify **one** scale used to measure volcanic eruptions. [1]

6   Suggest **two** secondary impacts that could occur after an earthquake. [2]

7   Suggest **two** factors that can influence the severity of the impacts of earthquakes. [2]

4.4 Managing the impacts of tectonic hazards

1   **a**   What is a primary response?

b   What is a secondary response?

c   Study Figure 4.7.

Figure 4.7: A primary response to an earthquake

What primary response to an earthquake is shown?

2 Draw a diagram to show how buildings can be protected from earthquake hazards.

3 How does planning help reduce the impacts of tectonic hazards?

4 Identify **one** primary response to a volcanic eruption. [1]

5 Identify **one** secondary response to a volcanic eruption. [1]

6 Using an example you have studied, suggest how the impacts of earthquakes can be reduced. [7]

UNDERSTAND THESE TERMS

- Primary response
- Secondary response

‹‹ RECALL AND CONNECT 2 ‹‹

Tectonic hazards can also be an attraction for tourists, bringing economic benefits to areas that are vulnerable to the impacts of volcanoes. See if you can answer the questions below from Topic 9, 'Economic change'.

a Suggest two factors that have led to the global growth of tourism.

b What is the difference between the primary and quaternary employment sectors?

c How does the employment structure of a high-income country (HIC) typically differ from that of a low-income country (LIC)?

SELF-ASSESSMENT CHECKLIST

Let's revisit the knowledge focus and exam skills focus for this topic.
Decide how confident you are with each statement.

Now I can	Show it	Needs more work	Almost there	Confident to move on
Describe the Earth's structure	State the name of the layer between the Earth's crust and core.			
Describe the processes and features of earthquakes and volcanoes	Draw a labelled diagram that shows a shield volcano and its features.			
Outline the impacts of tectonic hazards	Give three social impacts of an earthquake that you have studied.			
Evaluate the management of tectonic hazards	Discuss the view that earthquakes are easier to manage than volcanic eruptions.			

CONTINUED

Now I can	Show it	Needs more work	Almost there	Confident to move on
Understand the command word 'identify'	Answer an 'identify' question confidently, such as 'Identify one tectonic hazard associated with a transform/conservative plate boundary.'			
Understand the command word 'suggest'	Answer a 'suggest' question confidently, such as 'Suggest how planning can reduce the impacts of tectonic hazards.'			

5 Climate change

KNOWLEDGE FOCUS

You will answer questions on:

- 5.1 The natural and human causes of climate change

- 5.2 The impacts of climate change at a range of geographic scales

- 5.3 Responses to climate change

EXAM SKILLS FOCUS

In this topic you will:

- show that you understand the command word 'predict' and answer a 'predict' question

- show that you understand the command word 'assess' and answer an 'assess' question

- practise working with mark-scheme awareness.

When you are asked a 'predict' question, you need to suggest what may happen based on available information. This requires looking at patterns in data and using geographical knowledge to make a reasoned forecast. For example, if a climate graph shows rising temperatures and decreasing rainfall in a region, you might predict that droughts will become more frequent in the future. Your predictions should be realistic and supported by the evidence given.

'Assess' means to make an informed judgement about something. This involves considering different factors and weighing up their importance before reaching a conclusion. For example, if a question asks you to assess the effectiveness of international agreements in reducing climate change, you should examine both their successes and their limitations.

One of the best ways to improve your answers is by using mark schemes to check your own work. Marking your own answers helps you understand what examiners are looking for. Mark schemes can teach you how to properly answer the question, how to use the right geographical terms, how much to write and how to structure your answers clearly. This practice also helps you manage your time better in exams. The more you get used to using mark schemes, the more confident and accurate you will become in your answers.

5.1 The natural and human causes of climate change

1   Draw a diagram to show the differences between the natural greenhouse effect and the enhanced greenhouse effect.

2   Sort the following into natural and human causes of climate change:

   - changes to Earth's orbit
   - volcanic eruptions
   - burning fossil fuels
   - deforestation
   - sunspot activity
   - agriculture

3   What is the difference between climate change and global warming?

4   What are three pieces of evidence used to measure climate change?

5   Fill in the gaps with the correct words below.

   sea ice   paintings   ice cores   writings

   a   Scientists use _____ to study past temperatures by analysing gases trapped in ice.

   b   The position of _____ over time shows long-term climate changes.

   c   Historical records such as _____ and _____ provide evidence of past climate conditions.

When you are asked to predict and the question provides a source, such as a photo or a graph, remember to base your answer on the information provided.

6   Study Figure 5.1, which shows a cattle ranch in the Bolivian rainforest.

Figure 5.1: A cattle ranch in the Bolivian rainforest

Predict the likely factors contributing to climate change in Figure 5.1.   [2]

> **UNDERSTAND THESE TERMS**
>
> - Natural greenhouse effect
> - Climate change
> - Deforestation
> - Greenhouse gases
> - Enhanced greenhouse effect
> - Fossil fuel

7   Study Figure 5.2, which shows the total emissions of carbon dioxide and global temperature change between 1880 and 2018.

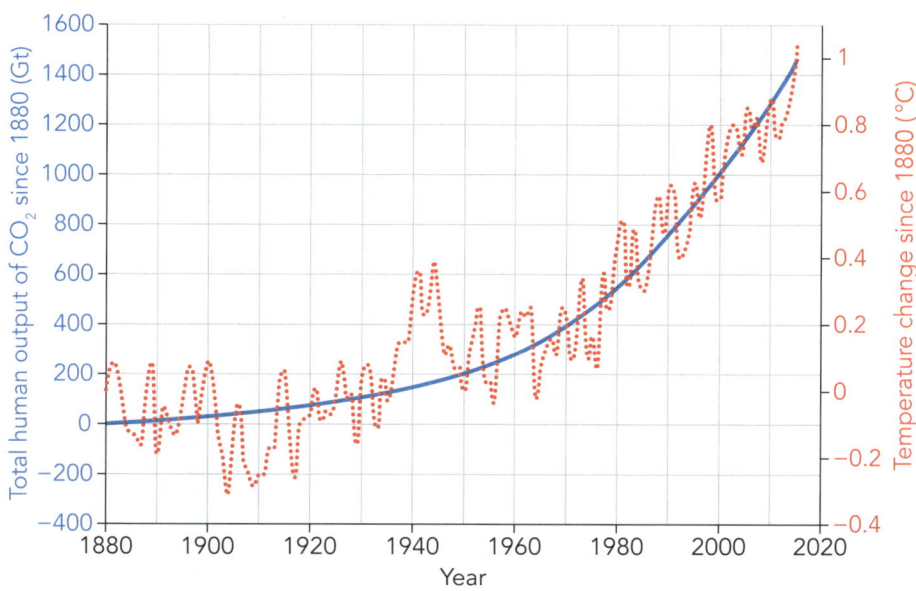

Figure 5.2: Graph showing carbon dioxide emissions and global temperature over time

Based on Figure 5.2, predict what will happen to global temperatures and carbon dioxide emissions in the future.   [1]

When you are asked to assess, remember this means making a judgement by weighing up both strengths and weaknesses.

8   Assess the role of different greenhouse gases in global warming.   [7]

9   Assess the extent to which humans are responsible for climate change.   [7]

REFLECTION

What helps you to remember the difference between the enhanced greenhouse effect and climate change? For example, you could remember that warming in a greenhouse is linked to an increase in temperature only (enhanced greenhouse effect) and that change can be positive and negative (climate change).

5.2 The impacts of climate change at a range of geographic scales

1   Fill in the gaps with the correct words shown below.

food production   sea levels   extreme weather events

a   Rising _____ are caused by melting ice caps and thermal expansion of the oceans.

b   Increasing frequency of _____ , such as hurricanes and heatwaves, indicate climate change.

c   Changes in _____ may lead to food shortages.

2   What is thermal expansion?

3   Decide if the following statements are true or false:

a   Some regions may experience stronger hurricanes and storms due to climate change.

b   Climate change only has negative effects on food production.

c   Rising temperatures can increase the spread of diseases such as malaria.

4   How might climate change contribute to an increase in climate refugees (people forced to leave their homes due to the impacts of climate change)?

> UNDERSTAND THESE TERMS
>
> • Drought
>
> • Thermal expansion
>
> • Climate refugee

When answering 'predict' questions that are not based on a source, such as a graph or photo, base your answer on your geographical knowledge and understanding. Make sure your prediction is realistic and clearly linked to what you know about the topic.

5   Predict **one** consequence of drought.   [1]

6   Predict **one** consequence of increased ocean temperatures.   [1]

7   Study Figure 5.3, a decile map which shows April to October rainfall between 2000 and 2021 in Australia. A decile map shows where rainfall is above average, average or below average for this period compared to all years from 1900. Predict the likely impacts of climate change for Australia.   [4]

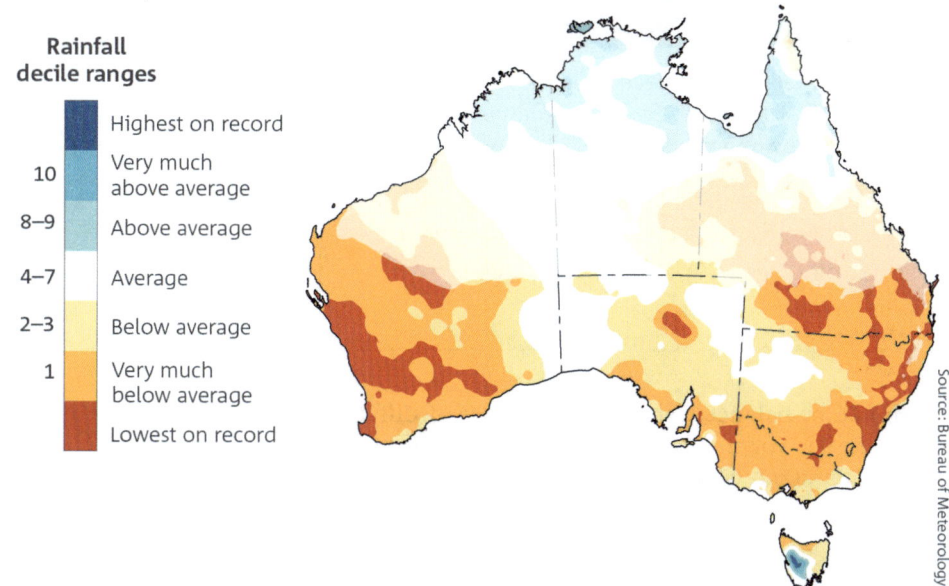

Rainfall decile ranges

	Highest on record
10	Very much above average
8–9	Above average
4–7	Average
2–3	Below average
1	Very much below average
	Lowest on record

Source: Bureau of Meteorology

Figure 5.3 April to October rainfall between 2000 and 2021 in Australia

---

≪ RECALL AND CONNECT 1 ≪

Climate change is a significant threat to Earth's ecosystems. See if you can answer the questions below from Topic 3, 'Changing ecosystems'.

a What is meant by the climate of an area?

b What are the factors that influence the characteristics of the Antarctic climate?

c How has one threat to the Antarctic ecosystem been managed?

d What are the layers of the tropical rainforest ecosystem?

e Why is the tropical rainforest climate so hot and wet?

f What are three threats to the tropical rainforest ecosystem?

5.3 Responses to climate change

1   How do international agreements and targets help mitigate the impacts of climate change?

2   What role does carbon capture and storage (CCS) play in combatting climate change?

3   What are two ways to adapt to the impacts of climate change?

4   Why is relocating coastal communities not always the best option when it comes to reducing the impact of climate change?

≪ RECALL AND CONNECT 2 ≪

Climate change will make urban areas a challenging place to live, especially as the population of towns and cities continues to grow. See if you can answer the questions below from Topic 7, 'Changing towns and cities'.

a   What is an unplanned settlement?

b   What is the difference between a brownfield site and a greenfield site?

c   What are the advantages of developing green spaces in urban areas?

d   What is urbanisation?

Your answer to an 'assess' question should be balanced, showing awareness of different viewpoints and the overall impact of the issue you are evaluating. Before answering these questions, use a mark scheme to understand what a Level 3 response to a 7-mark question includes.

Make sure you explain your points clearly and remember to include both advantages and disadvantages for each question. Look in the mark scheme for the types of key terms that you need to use and remember to include specific examples. Use examples of mark schemes to help you plan your answer so you stay focused and write the correct amount.

5   Assess the role of electric cars in mitigating the impacts of climate change.   [7]

6   Using examples you have studied, assess whether it is possible to adapt to the impacts of climate change.   [7]

REFLECTION

What makes a good response to an 'assess' question? For example, a good response should look at both sides of the argument before coming to a conclusion and could include the use of facts and figures. How could you improve your answers to 'assess' questions?

SELF-ASSESSMENT CHECKLIST

Let's revisit the knowledge focus and exam skills focus for this topic.
Decide how confident you are with each statement.

Now I can	Show it	Needs more work	Almost there	Confident to move on
Outline the natural and human causes of climate change	Explain the natural and human causes of climate change.			
Explain the effects of climate change	Suggest three impacts resulting from climate change.			

CONTINUED

Now I can	Show it	Needs more work	Almost there	Confident to move on
Assess the strategies to manage the impacts of climate change	Evaluate changing agricultural practices to help adapt to the impact of climate change.			
Understand the command word 'predict'	Answer a 'predict' question confidently, such as 'Predict the likely impact on climate change of clearing large areas of forest to make agricultural land.'			
Understand the command word 'assess'	Answer an 'assess' question confidently, such as 'Assess whether it is possible to reach "net zero".'			
Work with mark scheme awareness	Explain the key differences between a Level 1, a Level 2 and a Level 3 response for 7-mark questions.			

Exam practice 1

This section contains both past paper questions and practice questions. For each command word you have practised in Topics 1–5, you will find a past paper question or practice question with example student responses and commentary. You will then either improve the answer to the question using the commentary or answer similar practice questions putting what you have learned into practice. The questions draw together your knowledge and understanding of different geography topics and will help you prepare for your assessment.

Compare

In Topic 1, you explored how to approach the command word 'compare'. You learned that 'compare' means to identify or comment on similarities and/or differences between two or more features or concepts. These questions require careful reading to ensure you understand what is being compared. Remember, you can use key terms such as 'both', 'however', 'similarly' and 'in contrast' to help structure your answer effectively. You will now work through some example student responses to a 'compare' question and consider the right approach, before practising more questions using this command word.

1   Study Figure 1, which shows information about earthquakes between June and October 2019.

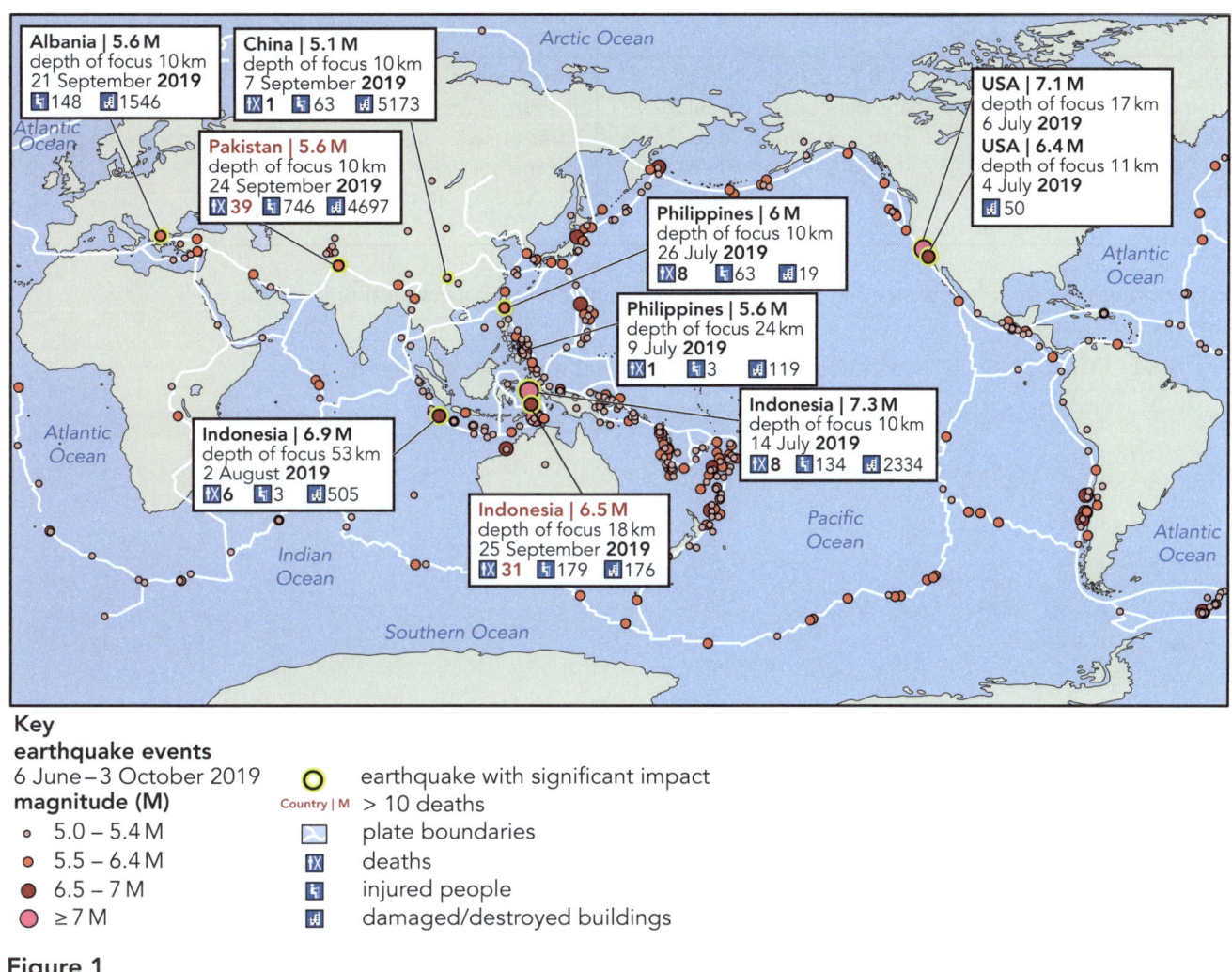

Key
earthquake events
6 June – 3 October 2019
magnitude (M)
- ○ 5.0 – 5.4 M
- ● 5.5 – 6.4 M
- ● 6.5 – 7 M
- ● ≥7 M

○ earthquake with significant impact
Country | M   > 10 deaths
▨ plate boundaries
Ⅸ deaths
☖ injured people
▥ damaged/destroyed buildings

Figure 1

Compare the impacts of the earthquakes in the Philippines on 9 July and 26 July 2019. [3]

Cambridge IGCSE Geography (0460) Paper 11, Q3a(iii), June 2023

Sample student response	Commentary
The earthquake on the 9th had a much deeper focus than the earthquake on the 26th. It also happened at a different time of year and in a different place.	The student makes three points. The points they make are about the depth of the earthquake focus, the date and the location, all of which are not about impacts. This means that they haven't answered the question.
The earthquake on the 26th had 8 fatalities, whereas the one on the 9th only had 1. This might be because of the time of day when the earthquake happened. There were also more injuries during the earthquake on the 26th. However, the earthquake in Indonesia had far more injuries than both of the ones in the Philippines.	The student gives two good differences between the earthquakes in the Philippines. However, they begin to suggest reasons for the differences, which isn't required when comparing the data on the map. This student then goes on to give a third point, but this time they refer to an earthquake in Indonesia. This is not a valid point to make because the question only asked about the Philippines.

Sample student response	Commentary
The earthquake on the 26th had 8 fatalities, whereas the one on the 9th only had 1. There were also more injuries during the earthquake on the 26th (63 compared to 3 for the earthquake on the 9th). Although more people were killed or injured on the 26th, there was more damage to buildings during the 9th July earthquake.	The student gives three clear comparisons between the two earthquakes mentioned in the question. Their answer is supported using accurate data from the map.

Considering the example answers, put what you have learned into practice with the following questions.

2   Study Figure 2, which shows information about the total world population since 1800 to 2025.

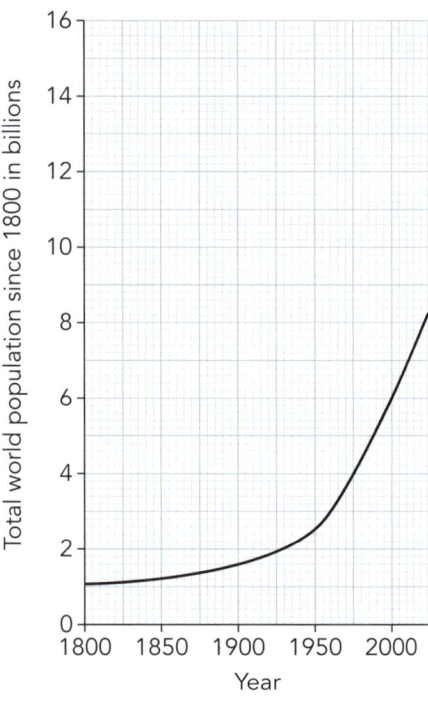

Figure 2

Compare the growth of the world's population from 1800 to 1950 with the growth between 1950 and 2025. Use statistics in your answer.   [2]

Adapted from Cambridge IGCSE Geography (0460) Paper 11, Q1a(ii), June 2023

3   Study Figure 3, which shows information about an eruption of Mauna Loa
     volcano in Hawaii.

Eruption of Mauna Loa

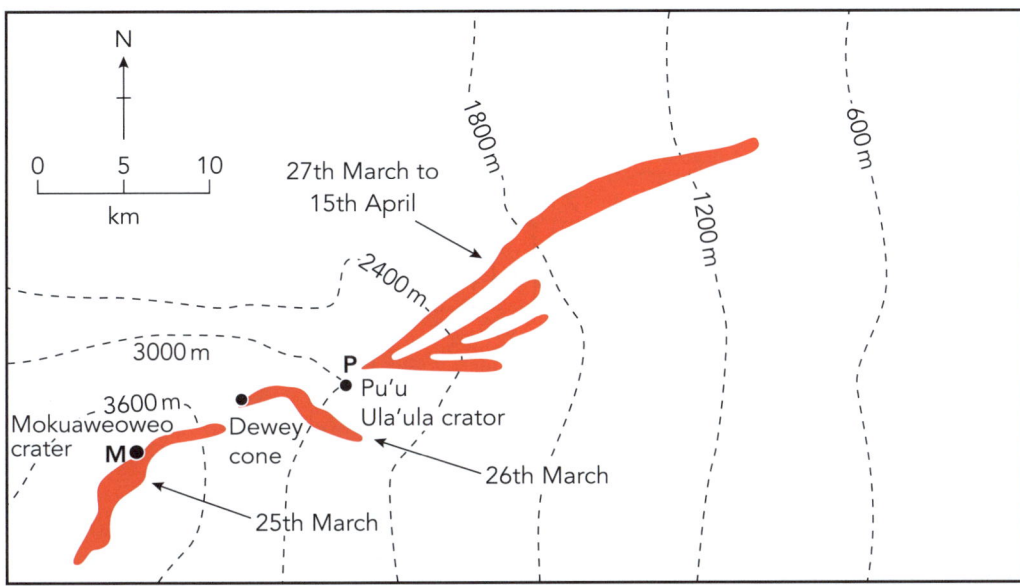

Key

   lava flow

- - - - - -   contour line

Figure 3

Compare the flow of lava from Mokuaweoweo crater (labelled M on Figure 3)
with the flow from Pu'u 'Ula'ula crater (labelled P).   [3]

Cambridge IGCSE Geography (0460) Paper 12, Q3b(i), June 2021

4   Study Figure 4, which shows climate graphs for McMurdo Station and Vostok in Antarctica.

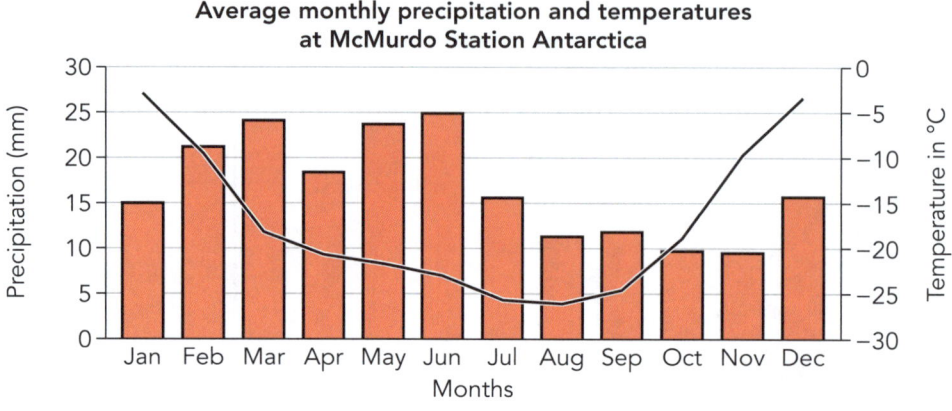

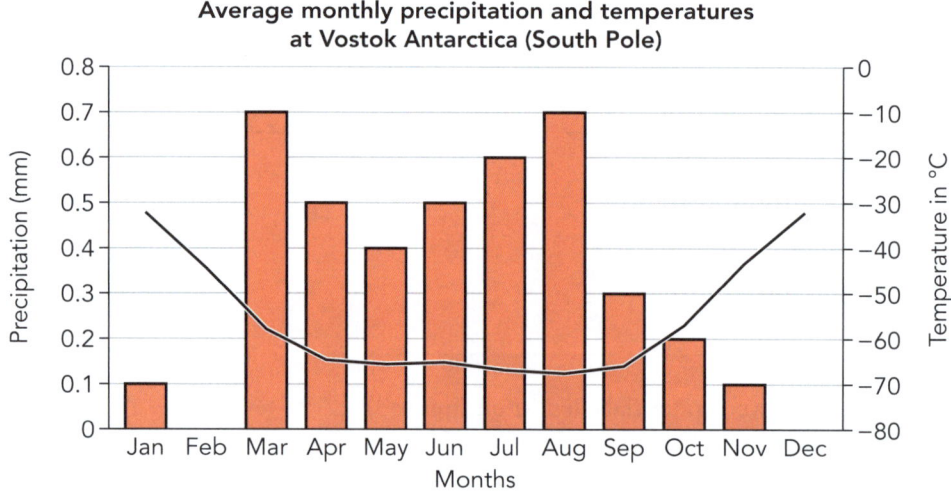

Figure 4

Compare the climate of McMurdo with that of Vostok.   [3]

Explain

In Topic 1, you also explored how to approach the command word 'explain'. You learned that 'explain' requires you to set out reasons or purposes, make relationships between ideas clear or say why or how something happens. You will now work through some example learner responses to an 'explain' question and consider the right approach, before practising more questions using this command word.

5   Explain how overgrazing may cause desertification.   [4]

Cambridge IGCSE Geography (0460) Paper 13, Q6a(iv), June 2022

Sample student response	Commentary
Too many cattle grazing in an area is called overgrazing. This can cause desertification.	The student defines overgrazing and says that it can cause desertification. The question didn't ask what overgrazing was, but rather how it may cause desertification. The response does say that overgrazing causes desertification, but it doesn't say how.
When there are too many cattle in one area, the plants can die, which leaves the land like a desert. When it rains, the land then washes away, and it is harder to grow more plants. The area is left like a desert, where nothing grows.	This response is better because it begins to explain the process of desertification and it makes the link between too many cattle, plants dying and the land becoming like a desert. However, it lacks depth and detail as it does not explain exactly how the land becomes a desert.
Overgrazing is when too many plants and grasses are eaten by livestock or when livestock trample vegetation and destroy it. This reduces the amount of vegetation growing, leaving the soil exposed to the wind and rain. When this happens, soil can quickly become eroded. Finally, the reduction in vegetation leads to lower levels of transpiration, which can lead to lower levels of rainfall. All of this means that semi-arid areas become more like deserts.	This response is detailed and uses key terms, such as 'eroded', 'transpiration' and 'semi-arid'. It accurately explains the process of desertification in a well-ordered manner. It also considers both the issue of soil erosion and lower levels of rainfall.

Considering the example answers, put what you have learned into practice with the following questions.

6   Study Figure 5, which is a photograph of a coastal area in Spain. Explain how the natural arch, marked Y in Figure 5, was formed by coastal erosion.   [3]

Figure 5

Cambridge IGCSE Geography (0460) Paper 11 Q3a(iii), November 2020

7 Explain how volcanoes offer opportunities to the people who live close to them. [5]

Cambridge IGCSE Geography (0460) Paper 11, Q3b(ii), June 2020

8 Explain why living on a delta or near a river may be hazardous for people. [5]

Cambridge IGCSE Geography (0460) Paper 11, Q3b(ii), November 2019

Describe

In Topic 2, you looked at how to approach the command word 'describe'. You learned that 'describe' means to state the points of a topic or give its characteristics and main features. You will now review some example learner responses to a 'describe' question before writing your own response to the question.

9 Describe **three** different characteristics of a coral reef. [3]

Cambridge IGCSE Geography (0460) Paper 12, Q3a(iii), June 2024

Sample student response	Commentary
• Coral reefs are in the sea. • They have fish swimming around them. • They are big.	This response is too vague and does not describe specific characteristics of coral reefs. Saying they are 'in the sea' is too general. The question asks for distinctive features. 'Fish swimming around' is not detailed enough to explain the role of coral reefs as a habitat. 'They are big' does not describe a specific characteristic.
• Coral reefs are made of calcium carbonate formed by tiny living polyps. • They are very colourful due to the presence of algae called zooxanthellae which live inside the coral and help them survive. • Coral reefs are found in warm seas.	This response contains two detailed descriptions of coral reef characteristics. However, the third point, 'Coral reefs are found in warm seas', is not sufficient because it does not describe a characteristic of coral reefs. Rather, it provides a fact about their location, which is not relevant to the question. When answering 'describe' questions, make sure to include enough detail to show your understanding.

Now write an improved answer to question 9.

Discuss

In Topic 3, you explored how to approach the command word 'discuss'. You learned that 'discuss' requires you to write about issue(s) or topic(s) in depth in a structured way. You will now work through some example learner responses to a 'discuss' question and consider the right approach, before practising more questions using this command word.

10 Discuss how rivers can be managed to reduce flood risk. [7]

Sample student response	Commentary
Rivers can flood, so people build things to stop water from going everywhere. Some places use walls to block the water, and some make the river bigger so it can hold more. Trees can help because they drink the water and people can stop building houses near rivers.	The student mentions some flood prevention methods, such as walls, making the river bigger, planting trees and not building near rivers. However, they do not use key terms like 'hard engineering' and 'soft engineering', or specific techniques like dams or channelisation. There is also very little in the way of discussion as they do not say how or why these methods reduce flooding. Some of the comments are very vague, for example, 'making the river bigger' is unclear. Does the student mean widening, dredging or something else?
Rivers can be managed to stop flooding. Hard engineering methods like dams hold back water and floodwalls stop rivers from overflowing. Channelisation makes water move faster. Soft engineering is better for nature. Trees (afforestation) soak up rainwater, and river restoration lets the river flow naturally. Floodplain zoning stops houses from being built where floods happen. These methods help to reduce flood risk.	This response covers both hard and soft engineering methods and also mentions different techniques like dams, floodwalls, afforestation and river restoration. They use simple language, making the answer easy to understand. However, this answer lacks depth as the student does not explain how the methods work in detail. There is also no evaluation, so they only discuss the positive aspects of the management technique.
Rivers can be managed using soft and hard engineering techniques. Hard engineering methods like dams and reservoirs control water flow but are expensive and can harm ecosystems. Channelisation straightens rivers to move water quickly, while floodwalls and embankments protect areas from rising water but may cause flooding downstream. Soft engineering works with nature and has less impact on the environment. Afforestation helps by increasing tree cover, which absorbs rainwater and slows runoff into rivers. River restoration allows rivers to flow naturally, helping to store excess water and reduce flooding. Floodplain zoning prevents building in high-risk areas, so fewer homes and businesses are affected by floods.	This response is well-structured into two paragraphs that use multiple key terms. The response is detailed, in that it explains how some of the techniques reduce the risk of flooding. This answer also acknowledges the benefits and drawbacks of management techniques.

Considering the example answers, put what you have learned into practice with the following questions.

11 Discuss the opportunities and challenges of living near the coast. [7]

12 Discuss the reasons why some earthquakes cause more damage than others. [7]

13 Discuss the role of mitigation (reducing emissions) and adaptation (adjusting to changes) when managing climate change. [7]

Sketch

In Topic 3, you also explored how to approach the command word 'sketch'. You learned that 'sketch' requires you make a simple freehand drawing showing the key features, taking care over proportions. Remember that you should start with a light outline and then add labels (short words or phrases that name or identify features of the sketch) and annotations (brief sections of text that describe or explain features and processes in more detail) to explain important features. You will now work through some example learner responses to a 'sketch' question and consider the right approach, before practising more questions using this command word.

14 Sketch a diagram to show the process of wave refraction.   [5]

Sample student response	Commentary
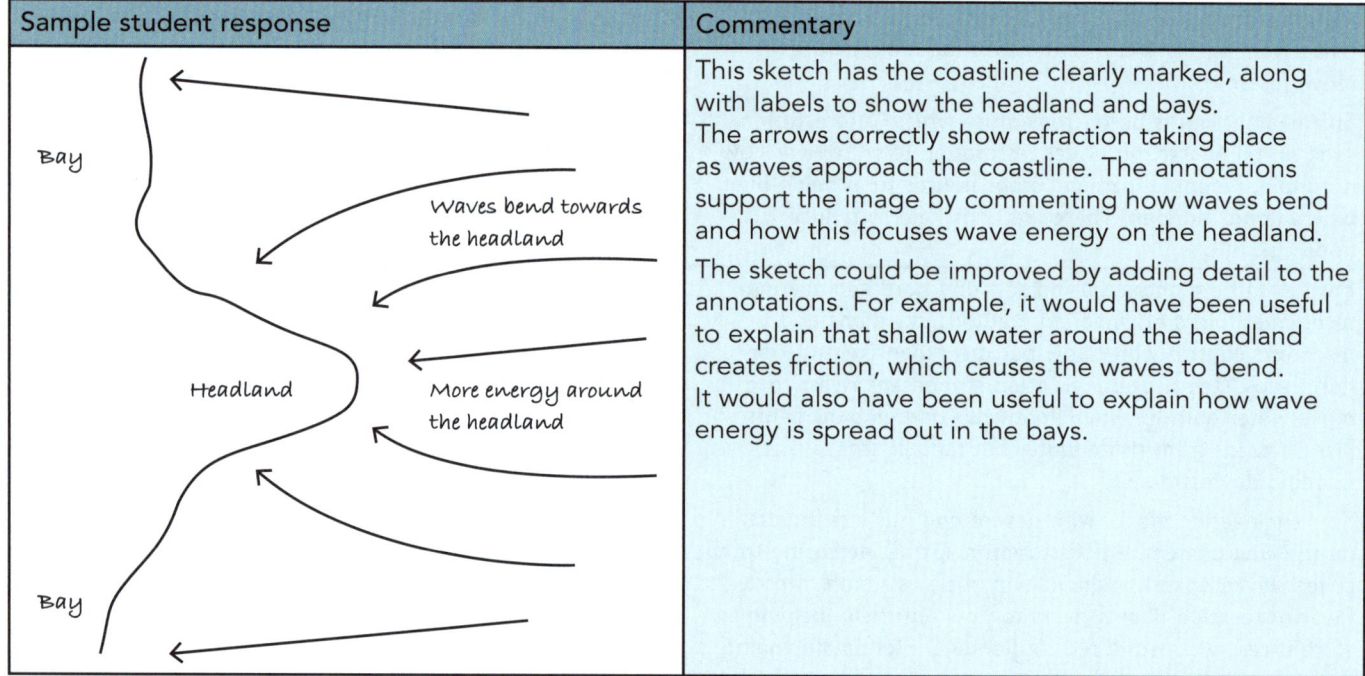	This sketch has the coastline clearly marked, along with labels to show the headland and bays. The arrows correctly show refraction taking place as waves approach the coastline. The annotations support the image by commenting how waves bend and how this focuses wave energy on the headland.
	The sketch could be improved by adding detail to the annotations. For example, it would have been useful to explain that shallow water around the headland creates friction, which causes the waves to bend. It would also have been useful to explain how wave energy is spread out in the bays.

Considering the example answer, put what you have learned into practice with the following questions.

15 Sketch a diagram or diagrams to show how oxbow lakes form.   [5]

16 Sketch a diagram of the landforms in Figure 6.   [5]

Figure 6

17 Sketch a diagram to show the features of a convergent and destructive
plate boundary.   [5]

Identify

In Topic 4, you reviewed how to approach the command word 'identify'.
You learned that 'identify' requires you to name, select or recognise something.
You will now examine some example learner responses to an 'identify' question
before writing your own response.

18 Study Figure 7, which shows an earthquake at a plate boundary.

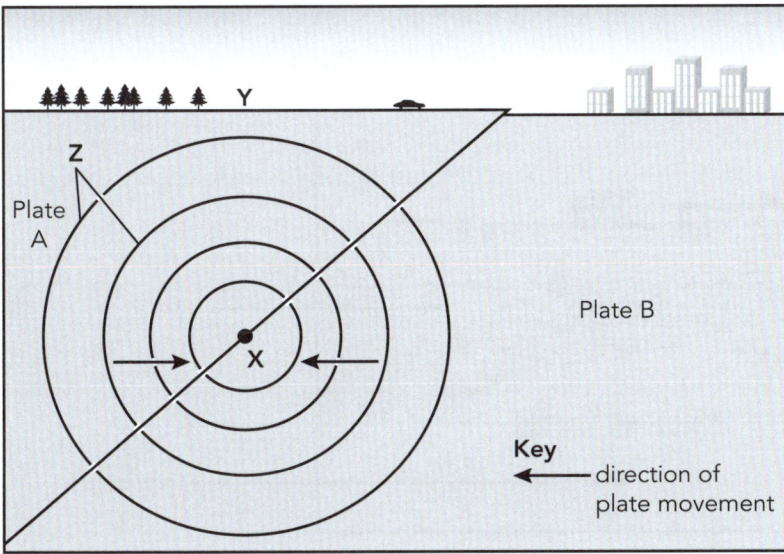

Figure 7

Identify the features labelled X, Y and Z on Figure 7.   [3]

Cambridge IGCSE Geography (0460) Paper 11, Q3b(i), June 2023

Sample student response	Commentary
X = Fault Y = Surface Z = Plate A	This response is too vague and does not accurately identify the key features of an earthquake at a plate boundary. The answer 'Fault' for X is incorrect because the diagram is labelling the point where the earthquake originates. The answer 'Surface' for Y is too general. It is referencing the precise point on the Earth's surface directly above the focus. 'Plate A' for feature Z does not describe the correct feature. This response lacks the precise terminology required for the question.
X = Epicentre Y = Focus Z = Energy	This response demonstrates some understanding of earthquake features but confuses key terms. 'Epicentre' for X is incorrect because X marks the point underground where the earthquake starts, which should be the focus. 'Focus' for Y is incorrect because Y is the point at the surface directly above the focus and should be labelled as the epicentre. This is a common mistake where the two terms are confused. 'Energy' for Z is too vague. Seismic waves do carry energy but the correct label should be seismic waves.

Considering the example answers, put what you have learned into practice with the following questions.

19 Study Figure 8, which shows a method of protecting the coast from erosion.

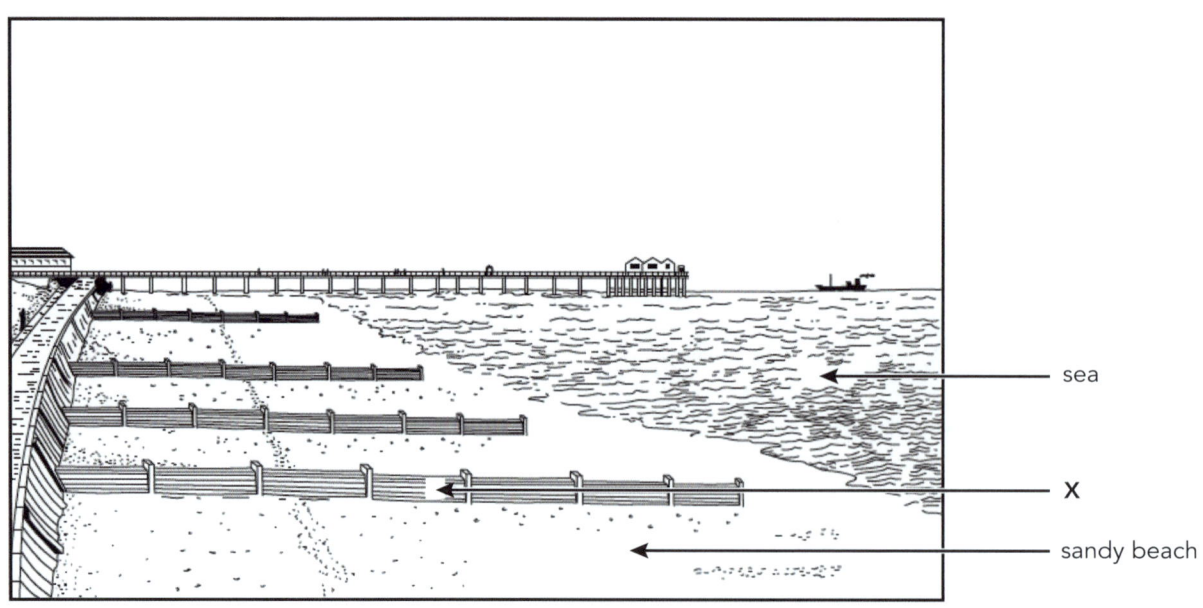

Figure 8

Identify the method of coastal protection which is labelled **X** in Figure 8. [1]

Cambridge IGCSE Geography (0460) Paper 11 Q3a(i) November 2022

20 Study Figure 9, which is an article about the world's hottest decade (period of ten years).

2010 to 2019 was the hottest decade on earth, according to recent data which also shows that 2019 was the second-hottest year ever. Nineteen of the hottest twenty years have occurred since 2000.

The annual global surface temperature is now increasing at an average rate of about 0.18°C per decade and every decade since the 1960s has been warmer than the previous decade.

Greenhouse gas emissions reached a record high in 2019 and the amount of carbon dioxide in the atmosphere is at the highest level ever.

Thirty-six countries, from Belize to South Africa, had their hottest year since records began. Many places around the world, including countries such as Switzerland, have had average temperate increases of more than 2°C over the past century. During December 2019 Australia experienced its hottest-ever day at 41.9°C and Europe recorded its hottest year ever.

Alaska also had its hottest year on record in 2019 with the ice melting during the winter in the Bering Sea. In the summer the temperature at Alaska's Anchorage International Airport reached over 32°C for the first time.

Figure 9

Identify from Figure 9 **three** different pieces of evidence to support the fact that global warming is occurring. [3]

Cambridge IGCSE Geography (0460) Paper 13, Q6b(i), June 2022

21 Study Figure 10, which is a diagram showing information about a tropical rainforest ecosystem in an area of equatorial climate.

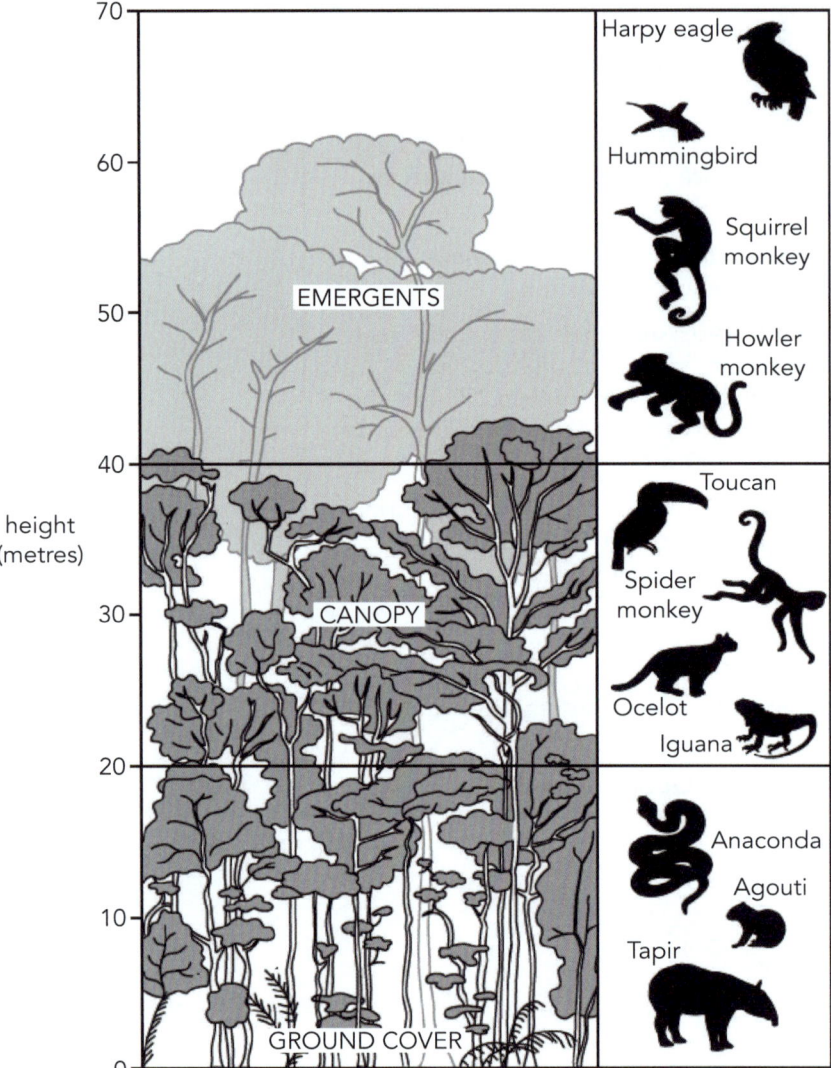

Figure 10

Identify from Figure 10, **one** example of:

- wildlife which lives in the canopy
- wildlife which lives in the ground cover. [2]

Cambridge IGCSE Geography (0460) Paper 11, Q4a(ii), November 2019

Suggest

In Topic 4, you also looked at the command word 'suggest'. You learned that 'suggest' involves applying knowledge and understanding to situations where multiple valid responses are possible, in order to make proposals, or put forward considerations. You will now analyse some example learner responses to a 'suggest' question and reflect on the best approach before practising further questions using this command word.

22 Study Figure 11, which shows information about earthquakes between June and October 2019.

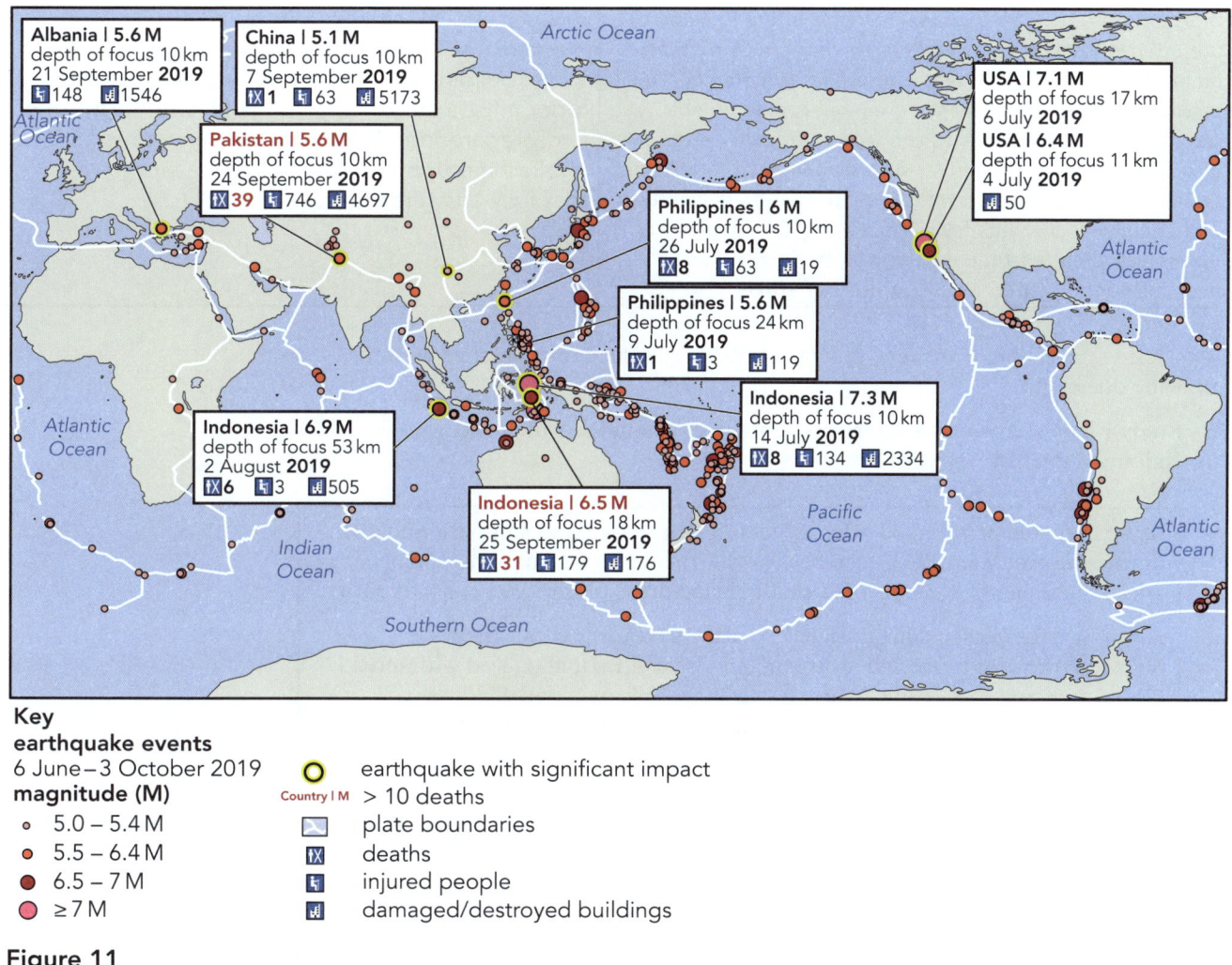

Figure 11

Suggest reasons why the earthquakes in the Philippines (an LIC) had a greater impact than the earthquakes in the USA (an HIC) between June and October 2019. [4]

Adapted from Cambridge IGCSE Geography (0460) Paper 11, Q3a(iv), June 2023

Sample student response	Commentary
The earthquakes in the Philippines had a greater impact than those in the USA because the country has weaker buildings that are not earthquake-proof, making them more likely to collapse. The Philippines may have fewer emergency services available to respond quickly to those affected.	The student correctly identifies two valid reasons why the impact in the Philippines was greater: 'weaker buildings' and a 'lack of emergency services'. They do not provide a more detailed explanation or additional points, though, such as issues with healthcare, emergency planning or access to aid. To answer the question more fully, the student should include more comparisons and more detail in their reasoning.
The earthquakes in the Philippines had a greater impact than those in the USA because buildings in the Philippines are often weaker and not earthquake-proof, making them more likely to collapse. There is also a lack of emergency services and healthcare meaning injured people do not receive quick treatment. This can lead to a higher number of deaths. Poor infrastructure, such as damaged roads, can prevent rescue teams from reaching affected areas quickly. The Philippines also has fewer emergency drills and lower awareness about earthquake survival, leading to more people being unprepared when a disaster strikes.	This response successfully explains four distinct reasons why the impact in the Philippines was greater than in the USA. It correctly references 'weak buildings', 'lack of emergency services', 'poor infrastructure' and 'lower levels of education and preparedness'. Comparative elements are also implied throughout. This makes it a strong response that fully answers the question.

Considering the example answers, put what you have learned into practice with the following questions.

23 Study Figure 12, which is information about earthquakes which occurred in Indonesia in 2018.

> More than 400 people died after a tsunami struck Java and southern Sumatra during the evening of 22 December. World Vision, an international aid agency, assisted families in some of the worst-affected areas on the west coast of Java.
>
> A few months earlier, a magnitude 7.5 earthquake struck Indonesia's Sulawesi province triggering a tsunami and landslides that caused widespread destruction and loss of life. More than 2000 people died and 4400 were seriously injured. With about 68 000 houses damaged or destroyed, hundreds of thousands of people were made homeless and without any income. Many communities were isolated due to damage to roads.
>
> The Central Sulawesi earthquake occurred less than two months after a series of earthquakes struck Indonesia's Lombok Island. The strongest of those earthquakes had a magnitude of 6.9. More than 500 people were killed and nearly 1500 were injured.
>
> The people affected by Indonesia's 2018 earthquakes and tsunamis will need help for years as they rebuild their lives.

Figure 12

Suggest **three** different types of help which would have been needed from international agencies, such as World Vision, after the earthquakes and tsunamis in Indonesia in 2018. [3]

Cambridge IGCSE Geography (0460) Paper 13, Q3b(i), November 2021

24 Suggest what could be done to reduce the impacts of future earthquakes on people in Indonesia. [5]

Cambridge IGCSE Geography (0460) Paper 13, Q3b(ii), November 2021

25 Study Figure 13, which shows information about the impacts of an earthquake in Italy, and Figure 14, a map of its location.

Emergency services are working in freezing conditions to find as many as 30 people feared trapped in a hotel in central Italy. It is now more than a day after the hotel was buried by an avalanche, as a large amount of snow slipped rapidly down the mountainside. The four-star Hotel Rigopiano, at the foot of the Gran Sasso mountain was covered by an avalanche of snow which is thought to have been triggered by an earthquake.

Despite the fear of further avalanches, rescuers battled blizzards and strong winds to reach the site. They had to ski for several kilometres in the darkness to get there because roads were blocked. Road crews had cleared much of the snow and fallen trees by the nighttime, finally allowing heavy rescue equipment to the hotel. Helicopters had earlier taken searchers, including dogs, up the mountain.

Figure 13

Figure 14

Suggest how the earthquake caused an avalanche of snow on Gran Sasso mountain. [2]

Cambridge IGCSE Geography (0460) Paper 13, Q4a(ii), June 2019

Predict

In Topic 5, you reviewed how to approach the command word 'predict'. You learned that 'predict' means to suggest what may happen based on available information. You will now examine some example learner responses to a 'predict' question and consider the correct approach before writing your own response to this question.

26 Predict how climate change may impact food production. [4]

Sample student response	Commentary
Climate change will make it harder to grow food. Some places will have more droughts and crops might not grow properly.	This response shows a basic understanding that climate change can negatively affect food production. It is too vague and lacks specific examples or detailed reasoning. The mention of droughts is relevant, but the answer does not explain how this impacts crop yields or food supply. To improve, the student should include more detailed points such as how temperature changes and shifting rainfall patterns affect different regions.
Climate change may impact global food production by increasing droughts in some areas, reducing water availability for crops. Rising temperatures could also make some regions too hot for traditional farming leading to lower crop yields. In contrast, some colder regions may experience longer growing seasons allowing them to produce more food. Extreme weather events, such as floods and hurricanes, may also damage crops and disrupt food supply chains.	This response provides three well-explained points: 'increased droughts', 'temperature changes affecting crop yields' and 'extreme weather disrupting food production'. The mention of 'longer growing seasons in colder regions' shows a balanced perspective, demonstrating that climate change does not only have negative effects but also positive impacts. To answer this 4-mark question, the student needs to add another well-developed point.

Now, write an improved answer to question 26.

Assess

In Topic 5, you also covered the command word 'assess'. 'Assess' means to make an informed judgement about something. You will now examine some example learner responses to an 'assess' question and consider the correct approach before practising further questions using this command word.

27 Assess the extent to which human activities contribute to climate change compared to natural factors. [7]

Sample student response	Commentary
Human activities contribute to climate change because people burn fuels like coal, oil and natural gas. This adds gases to the air which makes the Earth warmer. Some natural causes like volcanoes can also affect the climate, but humans are making it worse.	This response shows a basic understanding of the role of human activities in climate change by mentioning the burning of fossil fuels. It also briefly acknowledges natural factors such as volcanic activity. The explanation is too vague, though, and there is no discussion of how greenhouse gases like carbon dioxide and methane trap heat or how different human activities contribute to climate change. The response does not make an informed judgement about the relative impact of human and natural factors. To improve, the student should develop their explanations and use evidence for support, comparing human and natural causes in more detail.
Human activities, such as burning fossil fuels in industries and for transport release greenhouse gases like carbon dioxide and methane. These gases trap heat in the atmosphere, leading to rising global temperatures. Deforestation also increases climate change because fewer trees are available to absorb carbon dioxide. However, natural factors can also affect the climate. Volcanic eruptions release ash and gases which can temporarily cool the Earth by blocking sunlight. Changes in the Earth's orbit and solar activity also influence climate over long periods. Whilst natural causes have played a role in past climate changes, most scientists agree that human activities are now the main cause of recent global warming.	This response provides a more detailed explanation of how human activities contribute to climate change, mentioning specific sources of greenhouse gases and their impacts. It also acknowledges natural causes and therefore demonstrates a broader understanding. Although the response begins to compare human and natural factors, it does not fully develop an informed assessment as to the extent of their impact. To more fully answer the question, the student should explain why human activities have a more significant effect than natural factors today. The use of case studies or evidence would further improve the response.

Considering the example answers, put what you have learned into practice with the following questions.

28 Assess the effectiveness of international agreements in reducing the impacts of climate change. [7]

29 Assess the strategies and techniques being used to manage climate change in a named country you have studied. [7]

30 Assess the effectiveness of mitigation and adaptation strategies in managing the impacts of climate change. [7]

Human Geography

6 Population change

The command word 'calculate' means to work out from given facts, figures or information. 'Calculate' questions test your geographical skills and skills of analysis. If appropriate, remember to include units in your answer after you have completed your calculation.

To 'define' means to give a precise meaning. 'Define' questions test your geographical knowledge with understanding. You should be able to provide a definition for any of the key terms found in the syllabus. Flashcards are an excellent revision tool for learning the definitions of key terms.

6.1 Populations grow and decline

1 What is population momentum?

2 Fill in the blanks with the correct word(s):

    a The number of live births per 1000 people in a year is called the _____ rate.

    b When the death rate is higher than the birth rate, a population _____ .

    c Net migration is the balance between _____ and _____ numbers for a particular country.

3 Decide if the following statements are true or false:

    a The Demographic Transition Model (DTM) has four stages.

    b High death rates are common in countries in Stage 1 of the DTM.

    c A youthful population is associated with high fertility rates.

4 **a** Describe the challenges that a country in Stage 2 of the DTM may face.

    b What different challenges could a country in Stage 4 of the DTM face?

5 What is the main difference between a pro-natalist and an anti-natalist policy?

6 What is one strength and one weakness of the DTM?

≪ RECALL AND CONNECT 1 ≪

Development and population are closely linked. As a country's level of development changes, it affects birth rates, life expectancy and access to resources. See if you can answer the questions below from Topic 8, 'The challenge of development'.

a What is the difference between Gross Domestic Product (GDP) and Gross National Income (GNI)?

b Why are birth rates and death rates not reliable indicators of development when used on their own?

c How can international aid help reduce the development gap?

When answering questions that ask you to 'calculate', ensure you show all your working clearly and include appropriate units in your final answer (if appropriate).

7 Using Table 6.1, calculate the natural increase for that country. You may give your answer as a fraction or a percentage.   [2]

Crude birth rate	16
Crude death rate	10

Table 6.1: Measures of fertility and mortality for a country, per thousand per year

8   Table 6.2 shows world population growth over time.

Year	World population (billions)
1800	1
1927	2
1960	3
1974	4
1987	5
1999	6
2011	7
2022	8

Table 6.2: World population growth over time

a   Calculate how long it took to reach 2 billion people from the year 1800.   [2]

b   Calculate how long it took to reach 8 billion people from the year 2011.   [2]

9   A country's birth rate was 32 births per 1000 people in 2000. By 2020, the birth rate had decreased to 24 births per 1000 people.

Calculate the percentage decrease in the birth rate over this period. Show your working.   [2]

REFLECTION

Reflect on how you approach questions with the command word 'calculate'. Think about whether you double-check your calculations to avoid simple mathematical errors. How do you remember to include units?

UNDERSTAND THESE TERMS

- Population momentum
- Crude birth rate (CBR)
- Fertility rate
- Crude death rate (CDR)
- Natural increase
- Net migration
- Pro-natalist policy
- Anti-natalist policy

6.2 Population structures change over time

1   Draw a population pyramid for:

a   an ageing population

b   a youthful population.

2   Give some examples of factors that could cause 'indentations' on a population pyramid. Figure 6.1 shows an example of an 'indentation'.

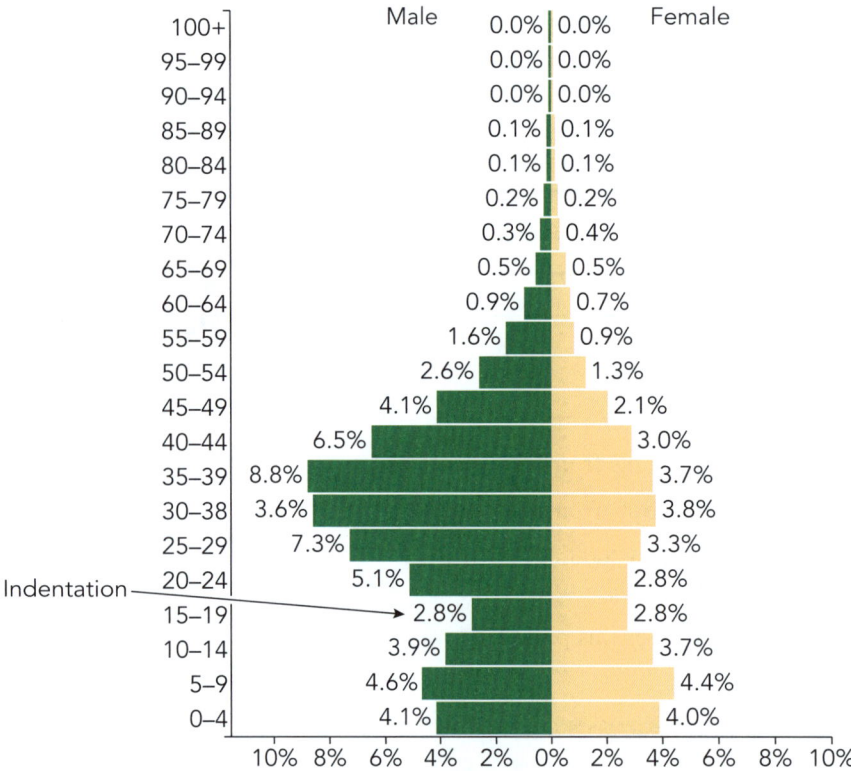

Figure 6.1: A population pyramid showing 'indentations'

<< RECALL AND CONNECT 2 <<

Growing populations impact the natural environment as urban areas expand to accommodate more people. See if you can answer the questions below on Topic 1, 'Rivers'.

a   Define the following key terms:

- Evaporation
- Interception
- Saltation
- Transpiration
- Percolation
- Traction

b   Using labelled diagrams, explain the formation of a waterfall.

c   Identify two hazards of living near a river.

When answering 'define' questions, you need to give an accurate definition of the key term in question. Try not to repeat the key term in your answer; instead, you may need to use synonyms (other words with the same meaning).

3   Define an ageing population.   [1]

4   Define population structure.   [1]

5   Define natural increase.   [1]

UNDERSTAND THESE TERMS

- Population pyramid
- Ageing population
- Youthful population
- Population structure

6.3 The causes and impacts of international migration

1   Match the definition, a–c, with the key term, 1–3.

1	push factor	a	The involuntary movement of people away from their home usually as a result of conflict or persecution.
2	remittances	b	Negative factors that encourage or force people to move from a place.
3	forced migration	c	The money or goods that migrants send back to families and friends in origin countries.

2   Copy and complete Table 6.3 by sorting the factors for migration into push factors or pull factors.

Factor	Push or pull factor?
war and conflict	
lack of education opportunities	
better job opportunities	
natural disasters	
access to healthcare	

Table 6.3: Push and pull factors for migration

3   Give two methods that governments could use to manage migration.

4   Define a refugee. [1]

5   Study Table 6.4 that shows the numbers of emigrants (people leaving a country) and the number of immigrants (people moving into a country) for Australia between 2023 and 2024.

Immigrants	Emigrants
667 000	446 000

Table 6.4: Number of immigrants and emigrants for Australia, 2023–2024

Calculate net migration for Australia, 2023–2024. [2]

UNDERSTAND THESE TERMS

- Push factor
- Pull factor
- Remittances
- Forced migration
- Refugee
- Net migration

SELF-ASSESSMENT CHECKLIST

Let's revisit the knowledge focus and exam skills focus for this topic.
Decide how confident you are with each statement.

Now I can	Show it	Needs more work	Almost there	Confident to move on
Give reasons for population growth and decline	State three reasons a country may experience falling birth rates.			
Describe and explain changing population structures	Explain why a country may experience an ageing population.			
Explain the causes and impacts of migration	Explain the impacts of migration on a country of origin you have studied.			
Understand the command word 'calculate'	Answer a 'calculate' question confidently, such as 'Calculate the natural increase for a country that has a crude birth rate of 7 and a crude death rate of 12.'			
Understand the command word 'define'	Answer a 'define' question confidently, such as 'Define crude death rate.'			

7 Changing towns and cities

KNOWLEDGE FOCUS

You will answer questions on:

- 7.1 Where people live
- 7.2 Opportunities and challenges of urbanisation
- 7.3 The management of urban growth

EXAM SKILLS FOCUS

In this topic you will:

- show that you understand the command word 'evaluate' and answer an 'evaluate' question
- show that you understand the command word 'state' and answer a 'state' question.

The command word 'evaluate' means to judge or calculate the quality, importance, amount or value of something. 'Evaluate' questions assess your ability to make reasoned judgements by analysing information, weighing up evidence and forming a conclusion.

The command word 'state' means to express in clear terms. 'State' questions are checking your ability to recall, select and communicate knowledge and understanding in a straightforward manner. 'State' questions typically require brief and direct answers.

7.1 Where people live

Some students ignore or misunderstand the command word 'evaluate' and instead write a description or explanation of something. You must respond to the command word in the question, so it is important you understand the difference between 'evaluate' and other command words. Look at the following questions to see if you can answer 'evaluate' questions.

1 Evaluate the extent to which push and pull factors contribute to urbanisation in LICs. [7]

2 Evaluate the challenges faced by cities in LICs due to rapid urban growth. [7]

REFLECTION

Do you understand the difference between 'evaluate' questions and other types of questions? In Questions 1 and 2, 'evaluate' means to consider different perspectives and make a judgement about the degree or importance of each. In other questions, evaluate can mean to discuss the strengths and weaknesses and come to a conclusion.

To reinforce your learning, try creating your own 'evaluate' questions based on what you've studied. This approach can help you develop a deeper understanding of the topic.

UNDERSTAND THESE TERMS

- Urbanisation
- Migration
- Natural increase
- Urban growth

3 Copy the following text and complete by choosing the correct word in the brackets.

In 2024, (**over/nearly**) half of all people lived in cities. It is estimated that by 2050, (**nearly/more than**) seven out of every ten people will live in cities. The number of megacities, which are cities with over ten million people, is increasing. (**Most/Few**) megacities are now in Asia, Africa and Latin America.

4 What are two causes of urban growth in LICs?

5 Push factors make people want to leave an area and pull factors encourage people to move to an area. In LICs, the direction of movement is often from rural to urban areas.

Sort the key terms from Table 7.1 into two categories: push factors from rural areas and pull factors to urban areas.

Lack of healthcare and schools
Extreme weather events that can destroy crops
Jobs that offer a higher rate of pay
Poor infrastructure: inadequate roads, transportation and communication systems
Higher standard of living
The 'bright lights' effect: the belief that life will be easier in cities

Table 7.1: Push and pull factors

UNDERSTAND THESE TERMS

- Push factor
- Pull factor
- Infrastructure
- Standard of living

7.2 Opportunities and challenges of urbanisation

'State' questions typically require concise and direct responses. Some students respond instead with lengthy explanations or descriptions. For 'state' questions, long descriptions or explanations do not make a stronger answer. Look at the following questions to see if you can effectively answer 'state' questions.

1   State **two** opportunities of urban living for residents in cities.   [2]

2   State **three** environmental challenges faced by cities due to rapid urban growth.   [3]

3   State **one** example of a social challenge caused by urbanisation in LICs.   [1]

4   State **one push** factor that drives people to leave rural areas for towns and cities.   [1]

REFLECTION

Do you recognise the difference between 'state' questions and other question types? Looking at Questions 1–4, you can see how 'state' prompts you to identify and recall specific information rather than describe or explain a concept. In this context, 'state' means to give straightforward answers without explanation or justification. Reflecting on this can help you become more precise in your responses.

How would the answers for Questions 1–4 look different if the command word was 'describe' rather than 'state'? Switching command words in this way can help to reinforce your understanding of the type of information required and improve your ability to differentiate between types of questions.

5   Give one environmental challenge associated with urban growth.

6   What is urban sprawl?

7   What challenges do cities in LICs face regarding the provision of services? Select the correct answer.

  a   low population density

  b   insufficient healthcare and education

  c   excessive funding for infrastructure

8   What is the difference between a brownfield site and a greenfield site?

UNDERSTAND THESE TERMS

- Brownfield sites
- Greenfield sites
- Urban sprawl

7.3 The management of urban growth

1   Match the key terms, a–d, with their definitions, 1–4.

a	Sustainable urban management	1	Urban management schemes planned by the government.
b	Top-down development	2	An urban management strategy that involves residents by providing them with building materials, tools and training that they use to construct and improve their homes.
c	Self-help scheme	3	Urban management schemes planned by small, non-government organisations often involving local people.
d	Bottom-up development	4	A city's use of resources and space in a way that meets the needs of its residents today without negatively impacting residents' needs in the future.

2   Green roofs and urban gardens are examples of green infrastructure. What do you think is meant by the term 'green infrastructure'?

« RECALL AND CONNECT 2 «

The growth of cities often leads to increased energy consumption and greater demand for transportation, which both generate carbon emissions and lead to climate change. As urban areas expand, there are also more impermeable surfaces and fewer green spaces, so less carbon is absorbed into the landscape. See if you can answer these questions linked to Topic 5, 'Climate change'.

a   State two human causes of climate change.

b   What is thermal expansion?

c   What is the difference between mitigation and adaptation?

3   State **two** challenges that urban planners face as a result of urban growth.   [2]

4 Study Figure 7.1, which shows information about the city of Stockholm. State **two** sustainable features of Stockholm. [2]

> Stockholm aims to be fossil fuel-free by 2045 and already generates most of its electricity from renewable sources, such as wind and hydropower. On a normal day, around 850 000 people use public transport, such as the underground metro system, electric buses and ferry services. Despite this, car traffic still contributes to air pollution. Around 90% of homes are connected to a district heating system, which heats homes using excess heat from industry and electricity generation. The city also has hundreds of parks and green roofs that help manage stormwater. Property prices in the city are higher than in other parts of the country.

Figure 7.1 Sustainability in Stockholm

5 Evaluate the effectiveness of congestion charging as a strategy to manage urban traffic. [7]

UNDERSTAND THESE TERMS

- Bottom-up development
- Congestion charge scheme
- Green infrastructure
- Self-help scheme
- Sustainable urban management
- Top-down development

SELF-ASSESSMENT CHECKLIST

Let's revisit the knowledge focus and exam skills focus for this topic.
Decide how confident you are with each statement.

Now I can	Show it	Needs more work	Almost there	Confident to move on
Explain where people live	State two reasons for rapid urban growth in LICs.			
Understand the opportunities and challenges of urbanisation	What are the opportunities and challenges of rapid urban growth and urban sprawl?			
Evaluate strategies for managing urban growth	How successful have strategies to manage urban growth been in a named area you have studied?			
Understand the command word 'evaluate'	Answer an 'evaluate' question confidently, such as 'Evaluate the extent to which building on brownfield sites is better than building on greenfield sites.'			
Understand the command word 'state'	Answer a 'state' question confidently, such as 'State two environmental challenges associated with urban growth in LICs.'			

8 The challenge of development

KNOWLEDGE FOCUS

You will answer questions on:

- 8.1 Measuring development
- 8.2 The world is developing unevenly
- 8.3 Achieving sustainable development

EXAM SKILLS FOCUS

In this topic you will:

- show that you understand the command word 'plot' and answer a 'plot' question
- show that you understand the assessment phrase 'to what extent' and answer a 'to what extent' question
- practise making connections between different topics.

The command word 'plot' means to mark point(s) on a graph/diagram/map. When responding to 'plot' questions, it is essential to present information clearly and accurately, using the correct scale, symbols or coordinates.

'To what extent' means to look at the degree to which something is true or accurate. 'To what extent' questions assess whether you can evaluate evidence, analyse information and form a balanced conclusion. To answer these types of questions, it is useful to present both sides of an argument before arriving at a conclusion.

This topic will also consider how to make connections across different concepts or topics. Making connections means recognising how different topics within geography link together, analysing patterns and making comparisons.

8.1 Measuring development

1 Match the following economic indicators of development, a–c to the correct definition, 1–3.

a Gross National Product (GNP)

1 The total value of goods and services produced in a particular country in a year.

b Gross Domestic Product (GDP)

2 The total value of goods and services produced in a particular country, plus income generated by its residents abroad in a year (it includes the income generated by citizens living abroad but excludes the income earned by foreign residents within the country).

c Gross National Income (GNI)

3 The total income earned by a country's people and businesses wherever in the world it is earned.

2 Identify the social indicators shown in Figures 8.1 and 8.2.

Figure 8.1: An example of a social indicator

Figure 8.2: An example of a social indicator

≪ RECALL AND CONNECT 1 ≪

As countries develop, their rates of urbanisation usually increase. This is because employment opportunities are frequently located in towns and cities and so rural-urban migration takes place. See if you can answer these questions linked to Topic 7, 'Changing towns and cities'.

a What is counter-urbanisation?

b Which type of country can be found at Stage 3 of the 'urbanisation pathway'?

c Which type of country is experiencing the fastest rates of urbanisation?

UNDERSTAND THESE TERMS

- Development
- Economic indicators
- Social indicators

When completing 'plot' questions, it is important to focus on accurately placing information on a map, graph, diagram or chart. These questions rarely require an explanation. Instead, you should ensure that each piece of information is plotted precisely and that it is visually clear.

3 On a copy of Figure 8.3, complete the graph by plotting the following information (see Topic 8 in the Resource Sheets):

- Saudi Arabia = 94%

- Morocco = 69% [2]

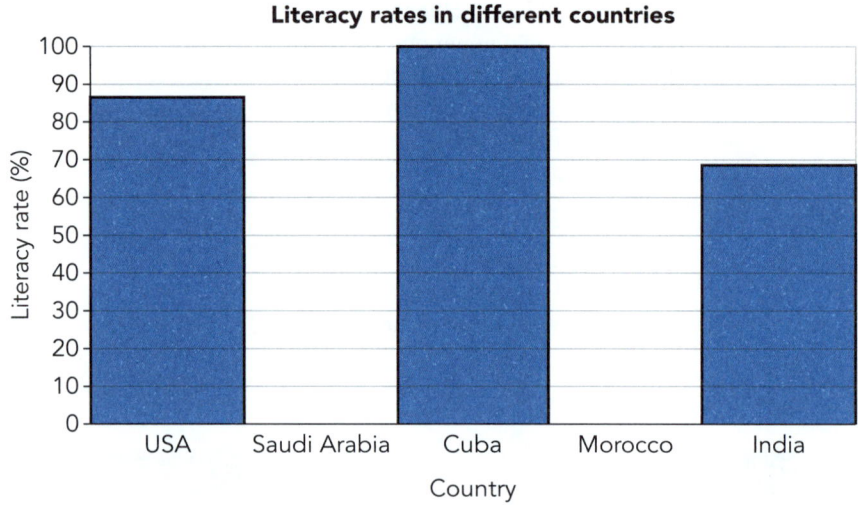

Figure 8.3: Literacy rates in different countries

4 On a copy of Figure 8.4, complete the graph by plotting the following information (see Topic 8 in the Resource Sheets):

- 2012 = 61

- 2022 = 66 [2]

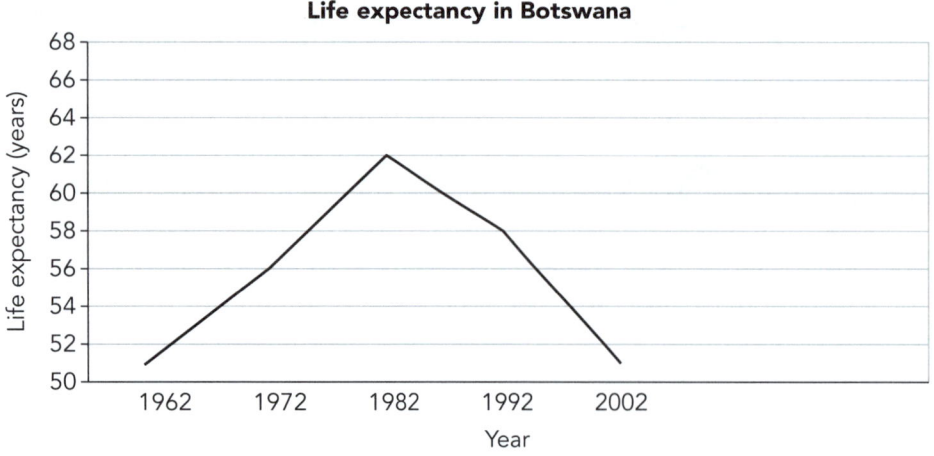

Figure 8.4: Life expectancy in Botswana

5   On a copy of Figure 8.5, complete the graph to show the following information about employment in Botswana (see Topic 8 in the Resource Sheets):

   •   % employment in agriculture = 18

   •   % employment in industry = 66

   •   % employment in services = 16   [1]

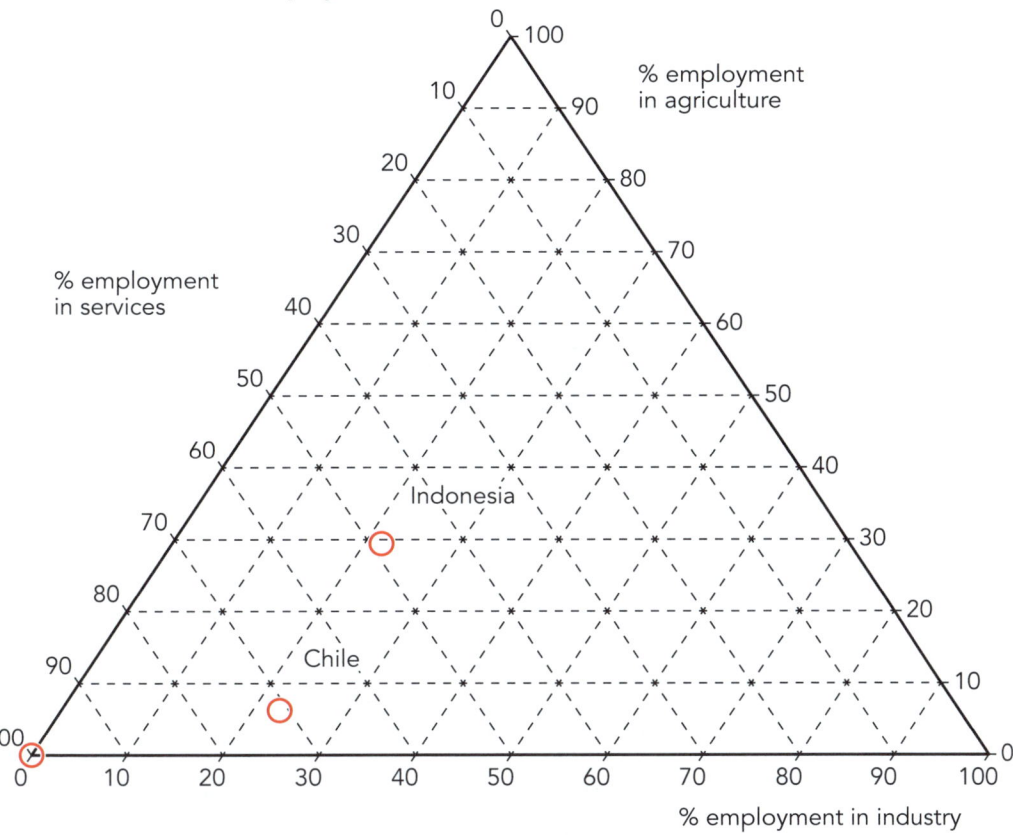

Employment structures in different countries

Figure 8.5: Employment structures in different countries

6 On a copy of Figure 8.6, complete the map to show the following information:

- Sudan = 63.2% of people have access to electricity
- Ghana = 85.1% of people have access to electricity   [2]

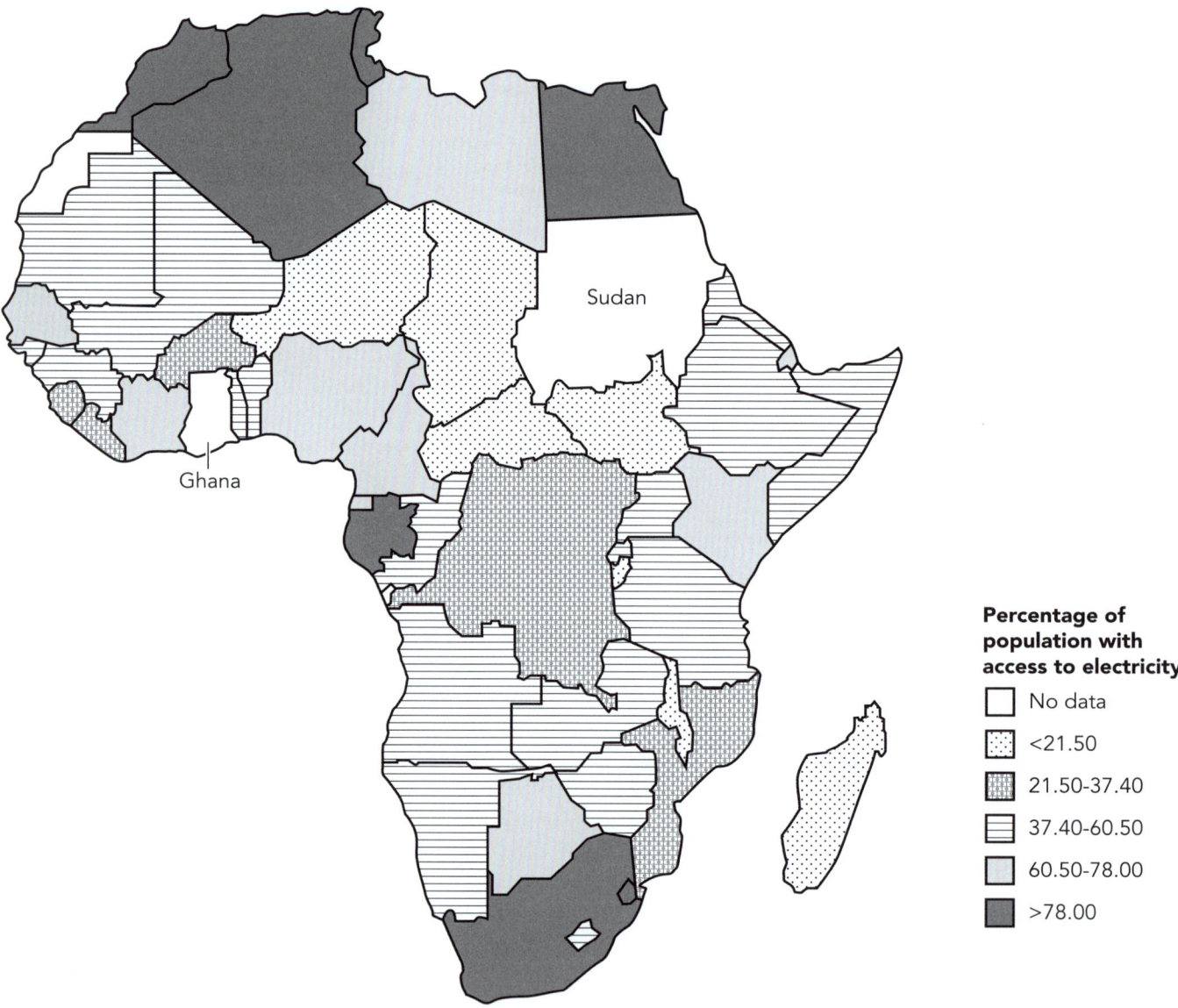

Figure 8.6: Access to electricity (% of population) in Africa

REFLECTION

Do you understand how 'plot' questions differ from other question types? In Questions 3–6, you practised accurately placing data including plotting literacy rates on a bar chart, life expectancy on a line graph, employment structure on a triangular graph and electricity access on a map. These questions did not require explanations or interpretations, but rather clear and precise presentation of data.

Consider what kind of data could be displayed on maps, charts, graphs or diagrams, and think about the types of questions that you need to be able to answer.

8.2 The world is developing unevenly

≪ RECALL AND CONNECT 2 ≪

Terminology to classify countries according to their level of income is also used in other topics in geography, such as population. See if you can answer the following questions about the classification of countries.

a Define 'HIC', 'MIC' and 'LIC'.

b Give examples of countries that are HICs, MICs and LICs.

1 The statements below outline reasons for uneven development. Sort the factors into three categories: economic, environmental and social.

a Colonialism slowed the development of the colony for the benefit of the colonising country.

b Trading primary products brings in less profit than manufactured goods.

c Countries with extreme climates may experience droughts and diseases such as malaria.

d Frequent natural disasters are expensive and disruptive.

e A good infrastructure can attract more foreign investment.

f Civil war can prevent a country from spending funds on essential services.

'To what extent' questions require you to judge how true or accurate a statement is. To do this, you must look at both sides of the argument: points that agree with the statement and those that disagree. Writing about something that contradicts the question is sometimes known as a counterargument. In these questions, it is important to show that you can look at evidence from different perspectives and make a balanced decision, rather than just giving a simple answer. After thinking about the different views, you should give a clear conclusion that explains your overall opinion.

Attempt these 'to what extent' questions by looking at both sides of the argument.

2 To what extent does climate determine a country's level of economic development? [7]

3 To what extent are natural resources essential for a country's development? [7]

4 Look at the sample answer to the following 'to what extent' question:
To what extent does unstable governance limit a country's economic development? [7]

1 This can reduce economic development.

2 However, unstable governance is not the only factor that affects economic development.

3 When governments are unstable, there is often a lack of clear policies, which makes it difficult for businesses to plan and invest confidently.

4 In conclusion, while unstable governance is a threat to economic development, its impact can be lessened through external influences such as trade and foreign investment.

5 In extreme cases, instability can lead to conflict or war, which disrupts economic activities and damages infrastructure.

6 Corruption takes money away from essential services such as healthcare and education.

7 Unstable governance can significantly limit a country's economic development by creating uncertainty, discouraging investment and weakening public services.

8 In addition to this, unstable governance can lead to corruption or the mismanagement of resources or money.

9 Other factors such as international trade, foreign aid or foreign investment from transnational corporations can overcome some of the problems caused by poor governance.

The answer has good elements, but it lacks structure. Put the statements into the correct order to produce an answer with a coherent structure.

REFLECTION

When you look at your answers to Questions 2–3, what do you notice about the structure of your responses? You may notice that the answers follow a similar pattern; one paragraph agrees with the question, another paragraph disagrees and then one paragraph gives an overall conclusion. Having a structure helps you to remember to include a counterargument.

8.3 Achieving sustainable development

1 Are the following statements true or false?

a The goals of the UN Sustainable Development Goals (SDGs) include ending poverty, addressing inequality and combating climate change.

b Aid guarantees positive outcomes for low-income countries.

c Trade contributes to development by driving economic growth and reducing poverty.

Making connections across different topics in geography is sometimes known as synoptic thinking. It involves recognising links between themes, identifying patterns and understanding how one concept can influence another. Here are some examples of connections between this topic and Topic 7, 'Changing towns and cities':

- Economic development can relate to environmental sustainability. Wealthier societies tend to use more resources, such as cars, personal technology or air conditioning, which generate pollution and drive climate change. Conversely, poorer societies tend to lack basic services, such as sewage systems and clean water. Both of these examples may lead to environmental damage.

- Changes in life expectancy can affect urban planning. Cities with more youthful populations require more amenities such as schools, whereas those with ageing populations may require more healthcare and supported living.

2 Evaluate the impact of rural-urban migration on the development of both rural and urban areas. [7]

3 To what extent does rapid economic development lead to environmental degradation? [7]

REFLECTION

Making connections will help you to see the bigger picture in geography, which can improve your overall understanding of the course. Making connections also enables you to form well-rounded answers when you answer questions. All topics within geography link to others. Try to think about what other synoptic links exist in this course.

Using a large piece of paper with the topics written on and drawing and labelling arrows between the topics is a good way to see the links. Do you think that this approach would help you to see the wider picture?

≪ RECALL AND CONNECT 3 ≪

Sustainable development can only be achieved if a country successfully manages its population. Too many people leads to overpopulation and too few people leads to underpopulation. Both scenarios can hinder development. See if you can answer the following questions linked to Topic 6, 'Population change'.

a What is fertility rate?
b What is natural increase?

---

4 Sort the following strategies into 'Top-down' or 'Bottom-up' development strategies:

- microfinance

- debt relief

- NGO-led projects

- UN Sustainable Development Goals

5   Fill in the blanks, using three terms from below:

bilateral   microfinance   debt   top-down   NGO

_____ relief is where organisations or governments cut or cancel a country's debt. This allows the country to invest in essential areas like healthcare and education.

_____ aid involves direct assistance from a donor country to a recipient country, often with agreements attached, such as the Akosombo dam project in Ghana.

_____ development strategies involve decision-making by governments or large organisations, often for large-scale projects, like building a hydroelectric dam.

> [!NOTE]
> **UNDERSTAND THESE TERMS**
>
> - Standard of living
> - Top-down development strategies
> - Bottom-up development strategies
> - Aid

SELF-ASSESSMENT CHECKLIST

Let's revisit the knowledge focus and exam skills focus for this topic.
Decide how confident you are with each statement.

Now I can	Show it	Needs more work	Almost there	Confident to move on
Explain how to define and measure development	How are countries measured and classified according to their level of development?			
Give social, economic and environmental reasons for uneven development	Name one social, one economic and one environmental reason for uneven development.			
Evaluate top-down and bottom-up strategies used to reduce uneven development	What are the advantages and disadvantages of top-down and bottom-up development strategies?			
Understand the command word 'plot'	Answer a 'plot' question confidently, such as those in Section 8.1 of this topic.			
Understand the assessment phrase 'to what extent'	Answer a 'to what extent' question confidently, such as 'To what extent does being landlocked limit a country's economic development?'			
Make connections between different topics	Make a list of synoptic links that can be found within this course.			

9 Economic change

The command word 'locate' means to indicate the position of a place, feature or entity from/in a resource. The resource could be a map, image or diagram. When locating the position of something, you must be as precise as possible.

The assessment phrase 'how far do you agree' requires you to make a judgement about whether you agree with something. 'How far do you agree' questions assess whether you can evaluate evidence, analyse information and form a balanced conclusion. The words 'how far' mean that you do not have to entirely agree or disagree, but instead you may agree or disagree to some extent. This command requires you to look in detail at a particular issue, considering both sides of the argument. This type of question will usually require an extended answer.

This topic will also consider what a good answer looks like. Knowing what a good answer looks like helps you to improve your own responses. Comparing your answers to example student responses allows you to see what you've done well and how you can make improvements.

9.1 Changing employment structures

1   Copy and complete Figure 9.1 to show the four sectors of the economy and examples of job types that fit within each sector.

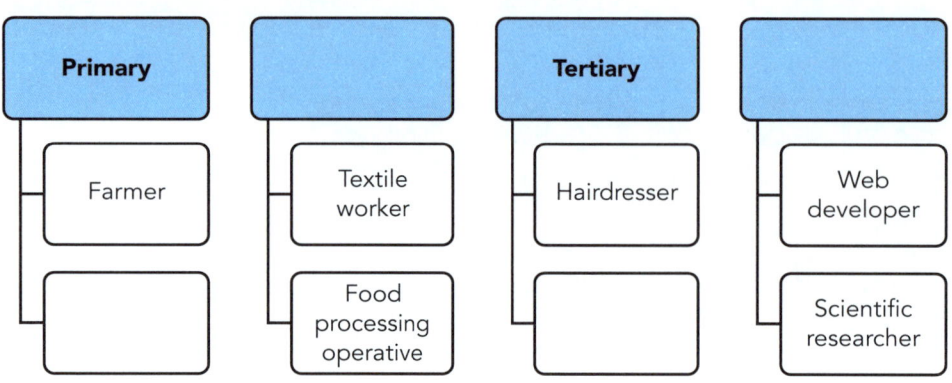

Figure 9.1: Classification of the sectors of the economy

2   The global industrial shift refers to the trend of manufacturing processes moving away from HICs to new industrialised centres. There are many factors involved in this global shift; some that make the transition to LICs easier and some that make it more challenging.

Match the following factors, a–e, to their explanations, 1–5.

Factors		Explanations	
a	labour	1	The availability of specialist machinery and reliable communications networks is important for most businesses.
b	containerisation	2	A skilled workforce at a comparatively lower cost increases profit.
c	technology	3	Time zones and spoken language vary between different countries.
d	political policies	4	Easier and faster transport and distribution of products makes it easier to move products between countries.
e	communications	5	Benefits such as tax exemptions or free trade zones reduce business costs.

3   Of the factors listed in Question 2, which typically make the global shift in industry easier (pull factors), and which make it more challenging (push factors)? Explain your answers.

REFLECTION

Sometimes, arranging facts in a different way encourages you to think more carefully about them. Diagrams, flow charts and tables can help us to remember information more easily than reading it as continuous text. Do the diagram and table in Questions 1 and 2 help you remember the content more easily? Do diagrams help you remember links between information and key facts and figures? Consider how you can use diagrams, flow charts and tables in your revision of this topic and others.

UNDERSTAND THESE TERMS

- Containerisation
- Global industrial shift
- Primary sector
- Secondary sector
- Tertiary sector
- Quaternary sector

≪ RECALL AND CONNECT 1 ≪

Economic changes within a country can influence government policies, such as those about population. For example, rapid economic growth can increase the demand for labour. If this happens, a government might implement policies to increase birth rates or attract migrants. See if you can answer these questions linked to Topic 6, 'Population change'.

a What is the difference between a pro-natalist and an anti-natalist population policy?

b Can you name a country that has implemented one of these policies?

Locating something is about accurately and precisely finding its specific position. Many people think about location as just being something that is found on a map, but this isn't always true. A question could ask you to locate something on a graph, or image, for example. Try the following 'locate' questions to see if you can accurately and precisely answer this type of question.

4 Study Figure 9.2, which shows the exports of goods and services (as a % of GDP) for Albania over time. On a copy of Figure 9.2, locate two points on the graph where significant decreases in the exports of goods and services (as a % of GDP) have occurred.   [2]

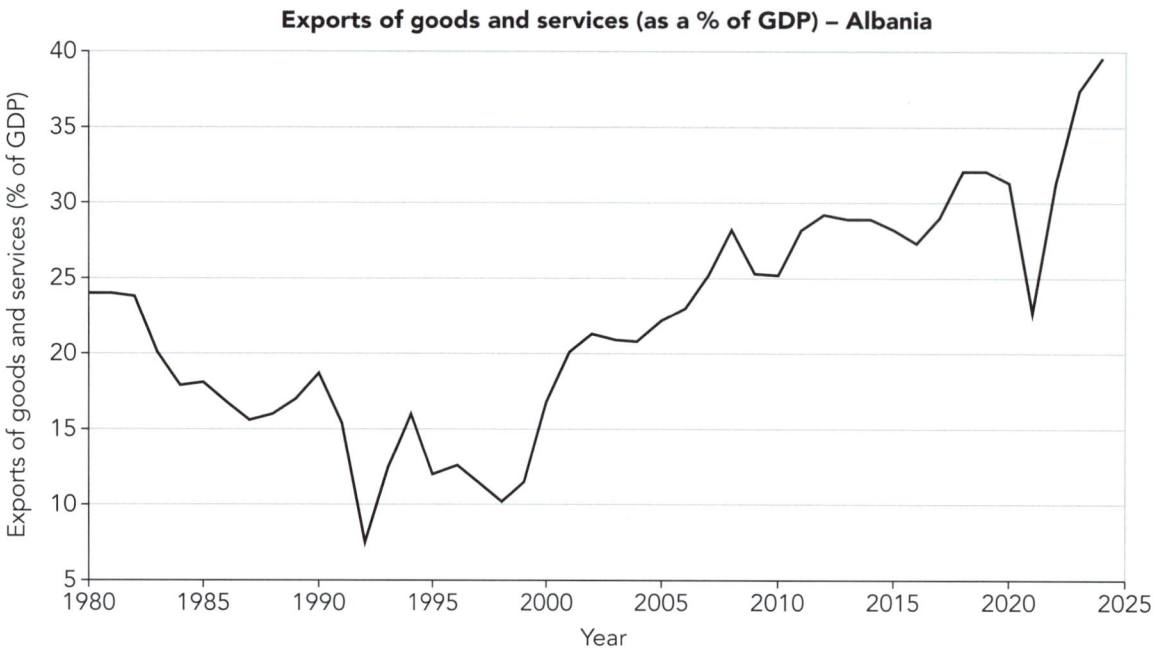

Figure 9.2: Exports of goods and services (as a % of GDP) – Albania

5   Study Figure 9.3, which shows Felixstowe, a town in the UK. On a copy of Figure 9.3, locate and label two types of structures or features that are related to industry (see Topic 9 in the Resource Sheets).   [2]

Figure 9.3: Felixstowe, UK

6   Study Figure 9.4, which shows Bakewell, a town in the UK. Describe the location of Lumford Mill.   [2]

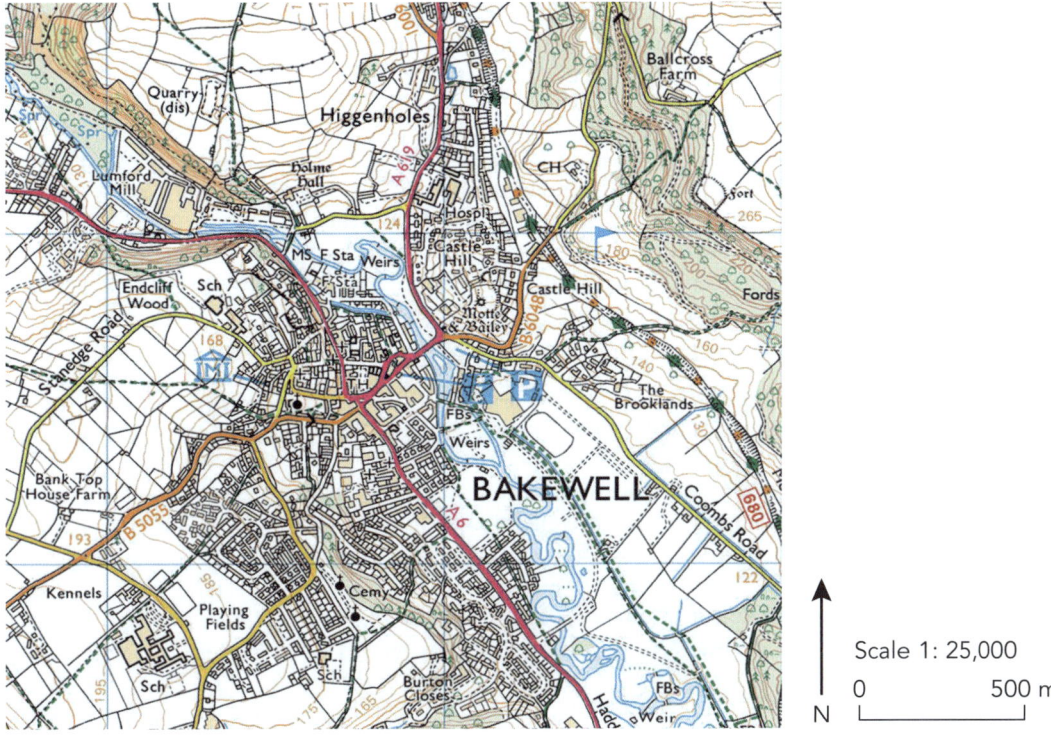

Figure 9.4: Bakewell in the UK

9.2 The impact of globalisation and the role of transnational corporations

1   List five impacts of globalisation.

2   Sort the following statements into economic, social and environmental impacts of transnational corporations (TNCs).

   a   Increased foreign investment in LICs.

   b   The movement of goods between countries increases carbon emissions.

   c   An increase in factories can lead to poor air quality.

   d   Increased revenue from taxes improves services such as schools and hospitals.

   e   Profits may largely end up back in HICs.

   f   Jobs are created in LICs.

   g   Some TNCs work to address gender inequalities.

   h   Some workers face unsafe working conditions.

   i   The global reach of TNCs means the impacts of any environmental improvement programmes can be far-reaching.

> **UNDERSTAND THESE TERMS**
>
> * Globalisation
> * Transnational corporations (TNCs)

When making decisions, geographers must consider all options and reflect on the views of others. This means that decisions are complex and there can be a spectrum of possible answers. The assessment phrase 'how far do you agree' acknowledges this by not asking for a definitive answer, but instead allowing you to say where you lie on that spectrum.

'How far do you agree' questions require you to make a decision, but you can say, for example, that you 'agree to some extent', or that you 'largely disagree', rather than fully agreeing or disagreeing. Other useful phrases to use with this type of question include 'it is partially true that', 'on the whole' or 'under certain circumstances'. These phrases allow you to show an awareness of the complexity of the question.

'How far do you agree' questions require explanation and so answers should be structured into paragraphs. A good way to do this could be to write a paragraph exploring reasons supporting your view, followed by another presenting counterarguments that you have considered. You may wish to finish with a short conclusion that confirms your position and addresses the question directly. A structure helps to ensure that your answer is clear, logical and well-balanced.

Try the following 'how far do you agree' questions:

3   'Globalisation brings positive economic impacts and negative environmental impacts.' How far do you agree with this statement?   [7]

4   'Transnational corporations (TNCs) do not benefit low-income countries.' How far do you agree with this statement?   [7]

> **RECALL AND CONNECT 2** <<

There are overlaps between this topic and Topic 8, 'The challenge of development'. See if you can answer these questions, which span both topics:

a   How do TNCs impact a country's level of development?
b   How can globalisation help to reduce global inequalities?

9.3 Tourism is a growing industry

It is beneficial to know what a good answer looks like. Recognising what makes an answer 'good' will help you to write better responses. First, answer the following questions.

1   Explain how tourism can affect the environment of a region.   [4]

2 Study Figures 9.5 and 9.6. Describe the negative impacts of tourism visible in the images. [4]

Figure 9.5: Tourists heading to Ed-Deir Monastery, a UNESCO World Heritage Site in Jordan

Figure 9.6: Tourists visiting the Great Pyramid of Giza, a UNESCO World Heritage Site in Egypt

Now you have answered the two preceding questions, look at the following example student responses to both questions. How could you improve these answers?

1 Tourism is bad for the environment as it can create pollution. In addition to this, people are employed in seasonal, poorly paid jobs. There can be a loss of culture as incomers demand food similar to what they're used to.

2 Negative impacts of tourism involve litter and noise. Tourists sometimes don't think about locals, and this can be offensive. Tourists can also bring benefits too, such as money and jobs.

If you need some help, think about the following:

- Question 1 asks about how tourism affects the environment. This means answers should only discuss environmental issues.

- Question 2 uses the words 'visible in the images'. The question does not ask you to talk about things you can't see, or to make assumptions about what you think tourists are like.

- Providing examples of positive and negative effects can give you answer balance and improve the amount of detail. Question 1 did not specify positive or negative effects, so you can discuss both. Question 2 only asked for negative effects, so you should not talk about positive effects here.

Now read the following stronger example student response to see what good answers to these questions look like.

1 Tourism can be both good and bad for the environment. The construction of secondary tourist resources, such as large hotels, roads and airports, can destroy habitats. Tourists arriving on aeroplanes and travelling in cars burn fossil fuels and contribute to carbon emissions. However, tourists can also mean that the environment of a place is protected. For example, tourists visiting a safari would encourage locals to protect the animals rather than hunt them. There is also a growing trend for ecotourism, which is a form of tourism that works to protect natural environments.

2   In Figure 9.5, there are a lot of tourists squeezing through small gaps in the rock, which may cause erosion. The monastery may also be a sacred site, and it could be disrespectful in some cultures to visit such sites in large numbers. In Figure 9.6, tourists are walking up the sides of the pyramid. This could damage the structure and could be seen by some as bad-mannered. Some tourists have their shoulders, legs and heads exposed, which can show a lack of respect in some cultures.

Now return to your answers to Questions 1 and 2 and improve them according to what you have learned about what makes a good answer.

REFLECTION
Can you see the differences between the first set of student responses and the second set? Student 1 hasn't read the questions properly. They have included answers that cannot be credited. For example, if a question asks you to identify things from an image, you should not list things that cannot be seen in the image! Which of the responses was most like your answers? Did you manage to improve your responses once you had seen what good answers look like?

UNDERSTAND THESE TERMS
• Ecotourism
• Primary tourist resources
• Secondary tourist resources

3   Put the following words into the correct place on Figure 9.7, showing the Butler Model:

• Involvement

• Decline

• Consolidation

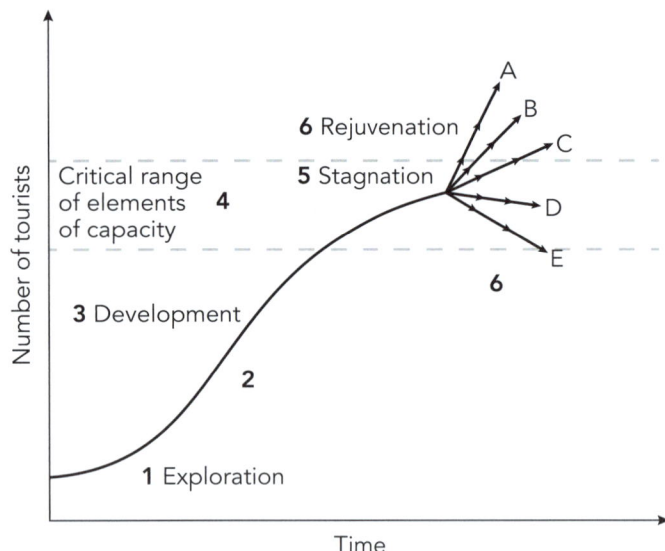

Figure 9.7: The Butler Model

4   Which stages of the Butler Model can be described as:

   a   a major change in direction or focus that happens to attract a new type
       of tourist.

   b   the tourist destination is well-known but is no longer a destination of choice.

SELF-ASSESSMENT CHECKLIST

Let's revisit the knowledge focus and exam skills focus for this topic.
Decide how confident you are with each statement.

Now I can	Show it	Needs more work	Almost there	Confident to move on
Describe how a country's economy changes as it develops	How do employment sectors of HICs differ from those of LICs?			
Explain the impacts of globalisation and the role of TNCs	What are the social, economic and environmental impacts of globalisation and TNCs?			
Identify the reasons for the growth in global tourism	What factors have led to the growth in global tourism?			
Explain the benefits and problems of global tourism	What are the social, economic and environmental impacts of global tourism?			
Understand the command word 'locate'	Answer a 'locate' question confidently, such as 'Locate a resort that is unable to compete with newer tourist attractions on the Butler Model.'			
Understand the assessment phrase 'how far do you agree'	Answer a 'how far do you agree' question confidently, such as 'How far do you agree that tourism has brought benefits to a country that you have studied?'			
Show that I understand what a good answer looks like	Look at some of your previous work that your teacher did not score highly. Re-write it to try and improve your original score.			

10 Resource provision

'Give' questions assess your ability to recall, select and communicate knowledge and understanding in a straightforward manner. For example, you may have to give a piece of data from a geographical data source or give a reason for something.

'Justify' means to support a case with evidence/argument. This could be when you are arguing for a certain point. For example, you may need to give reasons for the continued use of non-renewable energy sources, despite their impact on the environment and climate.

10.1 How food is produced

1 What are the three types of farming?

2 What are the differences between the three types of farming?

3 What are the two systems of farming?

When answering 'give' questions, ensure that you read the question carefully to identify what it is asking. It may be a one-word answer or a short sentence. It might be testing your recall skills or the use of a resource.

4 Give a physical input for a farming system.   [1]

5 Give **two** differences between commercial farming and subsistence farming.   [2]

6

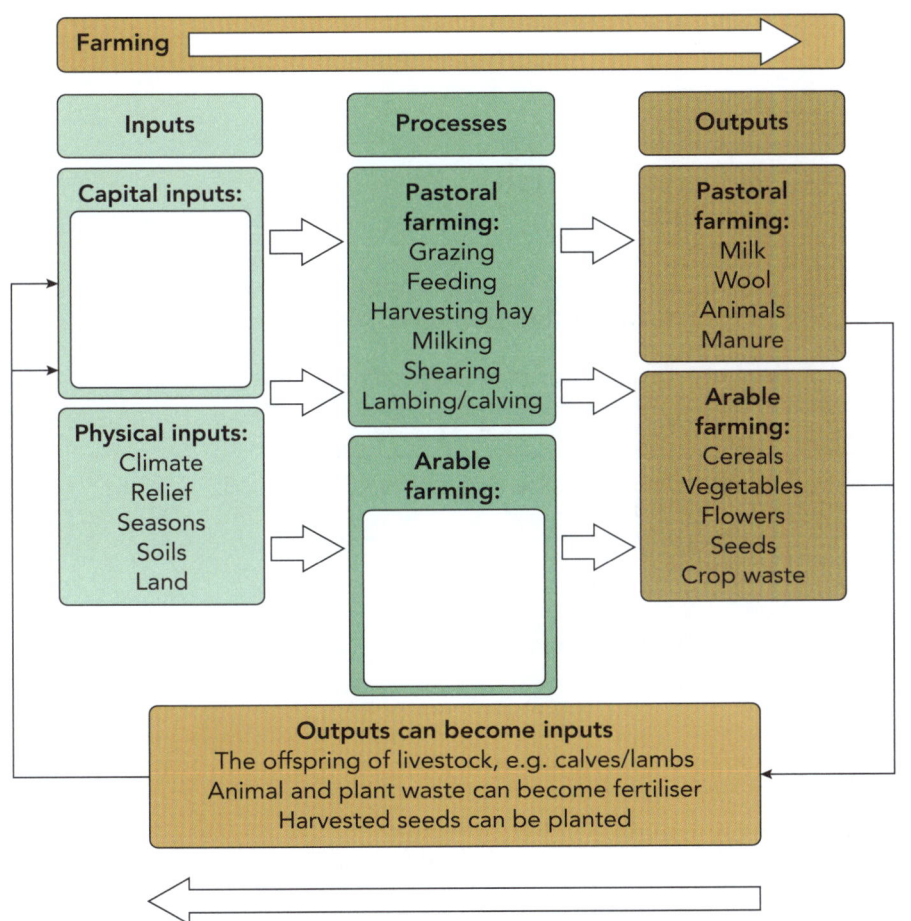

Figure 10.1: A flow diagram of a farming system

UNDERSTAND THESE TERMS
• Inputs
• Processes
• Outputs
• Aeroponics
• Aquaponics
• Hydroponics
• Arable farming
• Commercial farming
• Subsistence farming

Study Figure 10.1, which is a flow diagram showing the inputs, processes and outputs of farming systems. Using a copy of the diagram and then answer the following questions (see Topic 10 in the Resource Sheets).

a Add three capital inputs.

b Add four processes that arable farming could use.

7 Complete the sentences below.

   a Aeroponics is _____ .

   b Aquaponics is _____ .

   c Hydroponics is _____ .

REFLECTION

Aeroponics, hydroponics and aquaponics are all very similar sounding words. Do you have any strategies to help you remember the difference between them? For example, you could link the first part of aeroponics, 'aero', to the word 'aeroplanes' (which travel through the air) to help you remember that aeroponics is a technique of growing plants with their root systems suspended in air. Can you think of similar ideas for aquaponics and hydroponics?

10.2 The global patterns of food supply and demand

1 Table 10.1 includes strategies to meet food demand as well as their purposes.

irrigation	provides water to dry areas	increases crop resistance and yields
improves efficiency in farming	genetically modified crops	agricultural machinery

Table 10.1: Strategies to meet food demand and their purposes

   a Sort Table 10.1 into two columns: 'strategies for increasing food demand' and 'purposes'.

   b Match the strategy with its purpose.

2 What does the 'globalisation of food supplies' mean?

When you are asked to justify, you need to support your answer with clear reasons and evidence. This means explaining why a certain viewpoint or decision is valid, often by using your own knowledge or information from the question. Test your ability to justify by answering the questions below.

3 Justify the use of genetically modified (GM) crops to increase food supply.   [3]

4   Figure 10.2 shows the daily supply of calories per person in 2018.

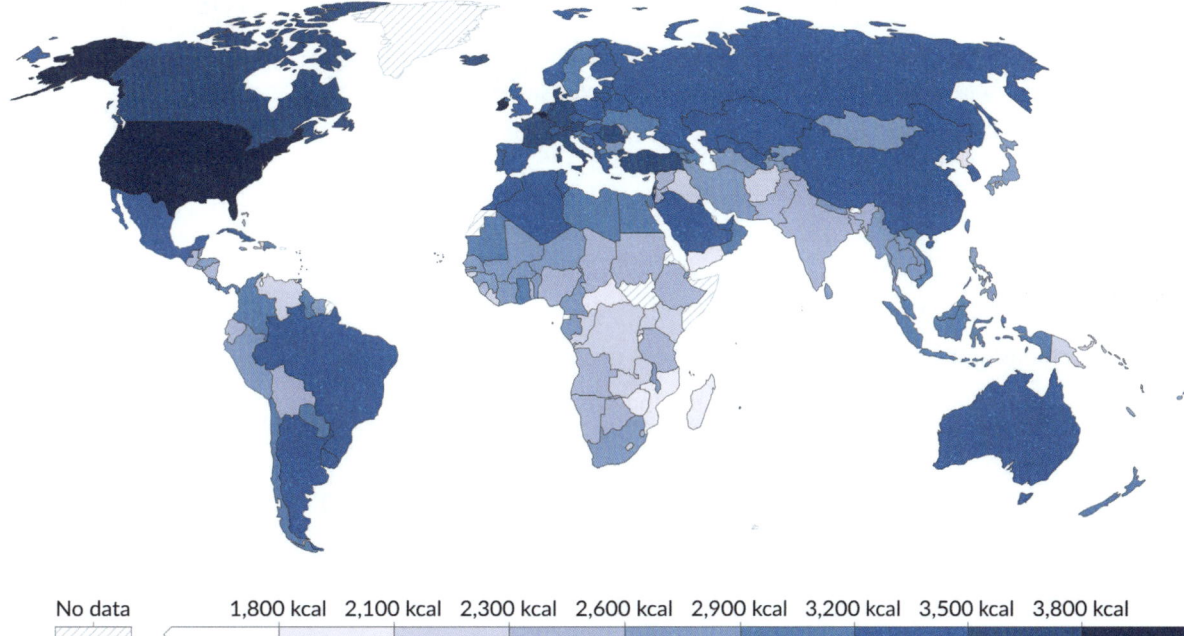

Figure 10.2: Daily supply of calories per person (2018)

Justify how increasing food production can help meet global demand.   [3]

10.3 The challenges of food supply

1   Study the factors affecting food supply in Table 10.2.

transport and storage	climate change	agricultural pests and diseases	war and political unrest
population growth	drought	demand for biofuel	land degradation and desertification

Table 10.2: Factors affecting food supply

Categorise the factors into 'human factors' and 'human and natural factors'.

2   Give **one** cause of desertification.   [1]

3   Give **two** ways human activity can lead to food insecurity.   [2]

4   Justify the use of food aid in reducing food insecurity in low-income countries (LICs).   [3]

5   Justify the use of strategies that reduce soil erosion.   [3]

6 How can food aid improve food security?

7 Identify a sustainable method to manage soil erosion.

≪ RECALL AND CONNECT 1 ≪

Growing populations put huge pressure on food resources on a local, national and global scale. Similarly to food supply, growing populations also face their own set of challenges. See if you can answer the questions below on Topic 6, 'Population change'.

a Describe the challenges that a country in Stage 2 of the Demographic Transition Model (DTM) may face.

b What different challenges could a country in Stage 4 of the DTM face?

c Explain how a high fertility rate affects the natural increase of a population.

d Identify one reason why a country might have high fertility rates.

e Suggest a method that a government could use to address the challenges of a rapidly growing population.

10.4 How our energy is produced

1 Energy can be generated from both renewable and non-renewable sources.

   a What is one example of renewable energy?

   b What is one example of non-renewable energy?

   c Why are fossil fuels considered non-renewable?

   d What is one advantage of wind energy?

≪ RECALL AND CONNECT 2 ≪

Energy can be generated from the heat under the surface of the Earth (geothermal energy). Geothermal energy is one of the positive impacts of volcanoes. See if you can answer the questions below from Topic 4, 'Tectonic hazards'.

a Copy and label Figure 10.3, showing the structure of the Earth.

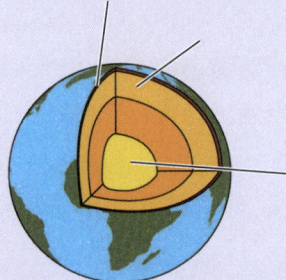

Figure 10.3: The structure of the Earth

≪ RECALL AND CONNECT 2 CONTINUED ≪

b Identify the plate boundary shown in Figure 10.4.

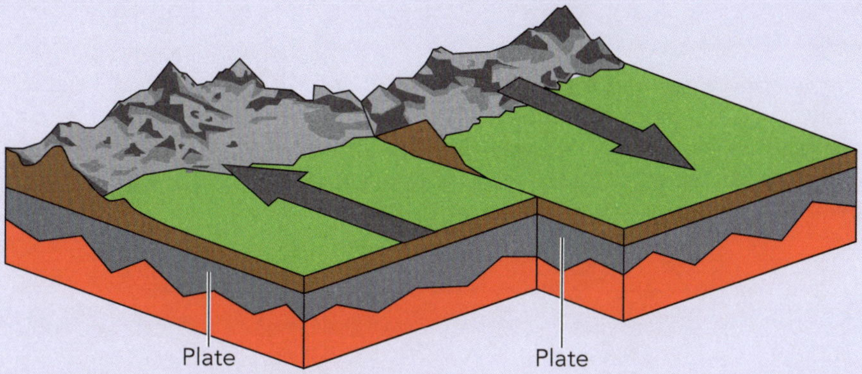

Figure 10.4: A plate boundary

c Describe the hazards associated with the eruption of a stratovolcano.

d Are the following statements true or false?
  i Oceanic plates are denser than continental plates.
  ii Continental crust is thicker than oceanic crust.
  iii Continental plates are younger than oceanic plates.

e How can buildings be protected from earthquakes?

2 Give **two** differences between renewable and non-renewable energy sources. [2]

3 Why is geothermal energy considered renewable energy?

4 Why can fuelwood be considered either renewable or non-renewable?

5 Justify the use of renewable energy sources. [3]

10.5 The global patterns of energy supply and demand

1 What is meant by the term 'energy security'?

2 What could make a country less energy secure?

3   Figure 10.5 shows the energy mix for Zimbabwe in 2022.

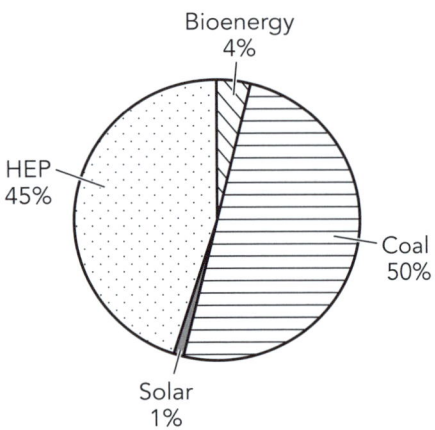

Figure 10.5: The energy mix for Zimbabwe in 2022

a   Give the percentage total of all the renewable energy sources.   [1]

b   Justify the use of coal in low-income countries such as Zimbabwe.   [3]

4   Why are HICs more likely to adopt renewable energy sources than LICs?

10.6 The impacts of energy production

1   Why is energy conservation important?

2   What is one way that individuals can save energy at home?

3   Give **one** positive impact of a secure energy supply.   [1]

4   Give **two** negative environmental impacts of renewable energy sources.   [2]

5   Justify the use of non-renewable energy sources.   [3]

REFLECTION

Having now completed a number of questions using the command word 'justify', what do you think makes the response below a good answer to the question? How will you approach 'justify' questions going forwards?

Justify how hydroponics can be a sustainable solution for food production in areas with poor soil.   [5]

Hydroponics is sustainable because it allows plants to grow without soil. This is done through the use of nutrient-rich water, making it ideal for areas with poor soil quality such as deserts. It uses up to 90% less water than traditional farming making it effective in water-scarce regions. Hydroponics can be done in urban or indoor spaces.

CONTINUED

This reduces the need for farmland and prevents deforestation. It also lowers the use of chemical pesticides and fertilisers reducing the impact on the environment. Hydroponics supports local food production, therefore cutting the carbon emissions linked to food transport and improving food security.

SELF-ASSESSMENT CHECKLIST

Let's revisit the knowledge focus and exam skills focus for this topic. Decide how confident you are with each statement.

Now I can	Show it	Needs more work	Almost there	Confident to move on
Describe how food is produced	Describe how aeroponics can be used to grow food.			
Outline global patterns of food supply and demand	Compare food consumption in HICs and LICs.			
Explain the challenges of food supply	Explain two human and natural factors that affect food supply.			
Describe how energy is produced	Identify three renewable energy sources and explain a benefit of each.			
Outline global patterns of energy supply and demand	What is meant by the term energy security?			
Evaluate the impacts and sustainable management of energy production	Evaluate the environmental impacts of burning fossil fuels to generate energy.			
Understand the command word 'give'	Answer a 'give' question confidently, such as 'Give one input used on an arable farm.'			
Understand the command word 'justify'	Answer a 'justify' question confidently, such as 'Justify the use of subsistence farming when there is a growing global demand for food.'			

Exam practice 2

This section contains both past paper questions and practice questions. For each command word you have practised in Topics 6–10, you will find a past paper question or practice question with example student responses and commentary. You will then either improve the answer to the question using the commentary or answer similar practice questions or past paper questions putting what you have learned into practice. The questions draw together your knowledge and understanding of different geography topics and will help you prepare for your assessment.

Calculate

In Topic 6, you reviewed how to answer questions with the command word 'calculate'. You learned that 'calculate' means to work out from given facts, figures or information. Remember that you should always show your working and include units where appropriate in your answers. You will now work through some example student responses to a 'calculate' question and consider the right approach, before practising more questions using this command word.

1   Study Figure 1, which shows information about population change in Norway between 1 January and 30 April 2013.

births	14 168
deaths	11 363
immigration	18 948
emigration	9319

Figure 1

Calculate the net migration for Norway between 1 January and 30 April 2013. You should show your calculations.   [2]

Cambridge IGCSE Geography (0460) Paper 11, Q1a(ii), November 2019

Sample student response	Commentary
Net migration is about people moving in and out of a country.	The student does not attempt the calculation required by the question. Instead, they provide a general definition of net migration. The question specifically asks for a calculation, so this answer is incorrect.

Sample student response	Commentary
9629	This answer is correct. However, there is no working out shown. Even if your calculation is correct, you need to show your working for a complete answer.
18 948 − 9319 = 9629	This answer is correct because it demonstrates the calculation involved and presents the final answer clearly.

Considering the example answers, put what you have learned into practice with the following questions.

2 Study Figure 2, which shows information about birth rates and death rates in China between 1950 and 2020.

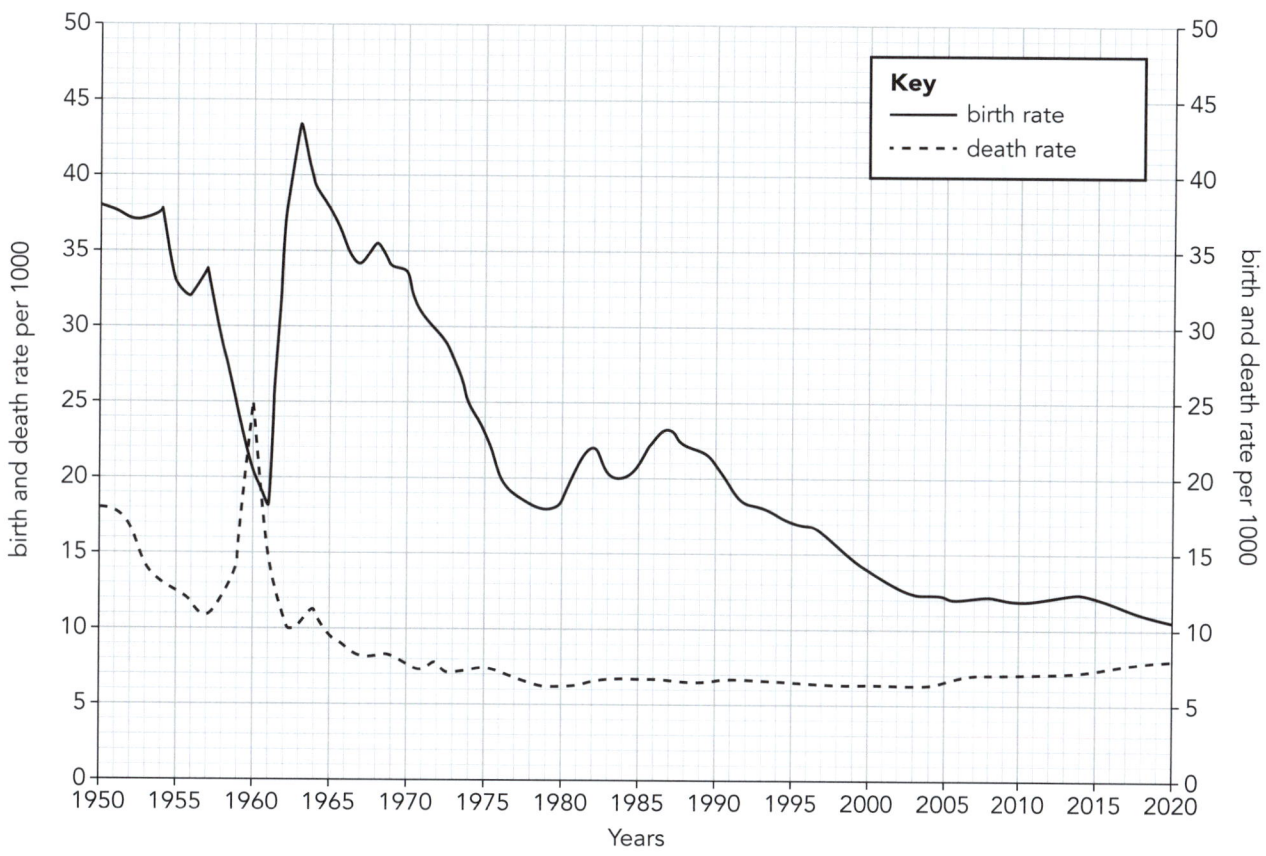

Figure 2

Using Figure 2, calculate the reduction in the natural population growth rate of China between 1950 and 2020 per 1000. You should show your calculations. [3]

Adapted from Cambridge IGCSE Geography (0460) Paper 11, Q1a(iii), November 2022

3 Study Figure 3, which shows information about agriculture in Pakistan, an LIC in Asia. Calculate the area by which arable land increased in Pakistan between 1950 and 2010. [1]

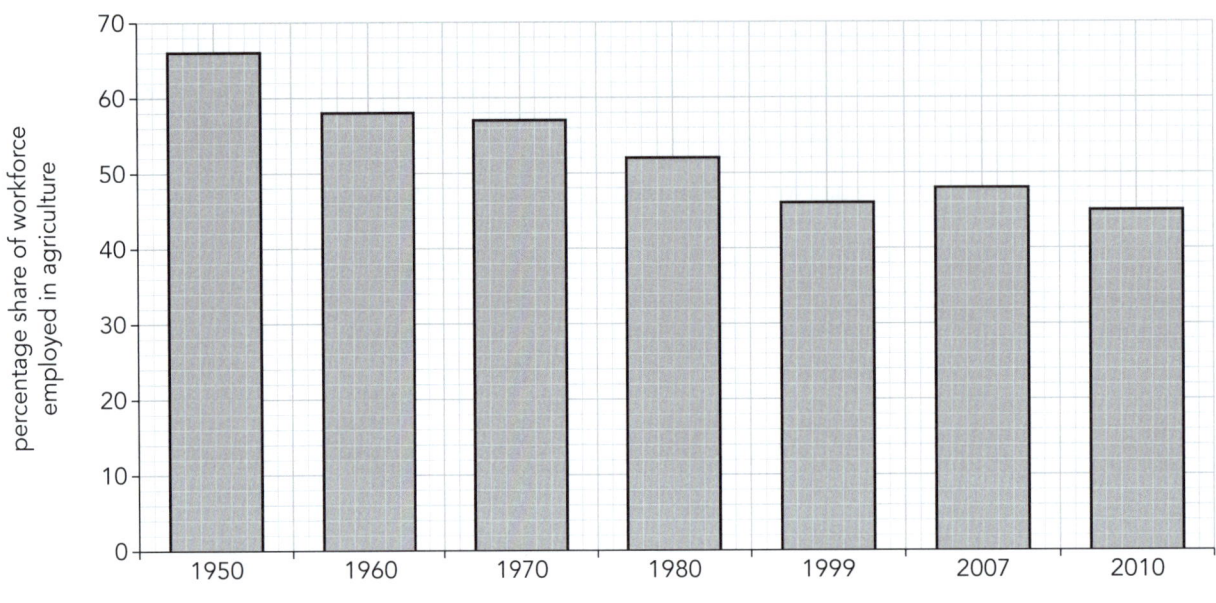

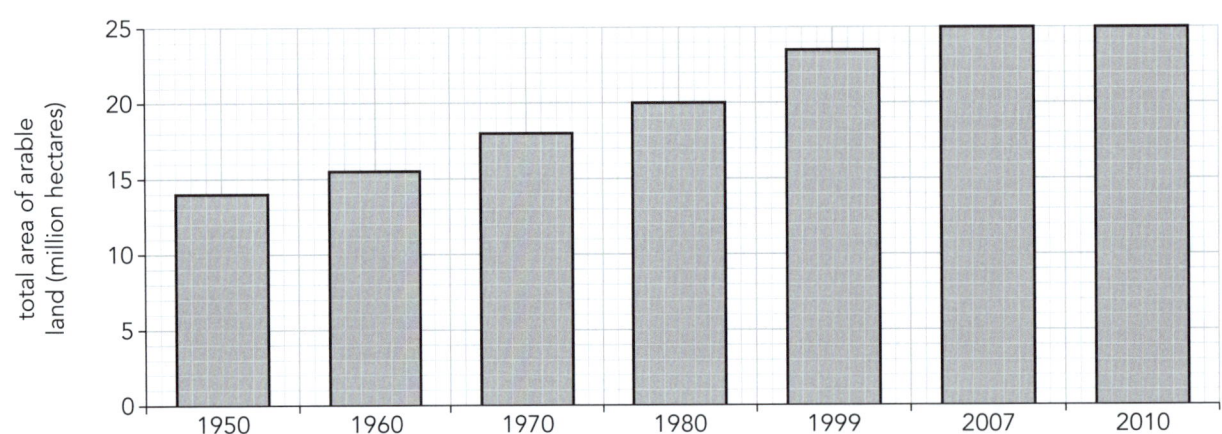

Figure 3

Adapted from Cambridge IGCSE Geography (0460) Paper 11, Q5a(i), June 2020

4 In 2000, 60% of workers in Country A were employed in primary and secondary industries. By 2020, this had fallen to 35%. The total workforce in 2020 was 20 million.

Calculate how many fewer people were working in primary and secondary industries in 2020 compared to 2000. You should show your calculations. [2]

Define

You also reviewed the command word 'define' in Topic 6. 'Define' means to give a precise meaning of something. This assesses your geographical knowledge and understanding. Remember, you should be able to provide a definition for any of the key terms found in the Coursebook.

5 Define the following types of migrant:

- economic migrant

- asylum seeker

- refugee   [3]

Sample student response	Commentary
An economic migrant is someone looking for work. An asylum seeker is a person asking for help in another country. A refugee is someone who has escaped danger in their country.	The definitions are too vague and miss key details. For example, 'looking for work' should specify moving to another country, and 'asking for help' does not clearly explain that asylum seekers seek international protection and are not yet recognised as refugees. 'Escaped danger' is too broad to define a refugee, as it does not mention persecution or conflict. This response shows basic understanding but lacks accurate definitions to the key terms in the question.

Now write an improved answer to Question 5.

Evaluate

In Topic 7, you reviewed how to approach the 'evaluate' command word. You learned that 'evaluate' means to judge or calculate the quality, importance, amount or value of something. You should avoid simply describing or explaining; instead, focus on analysing evidence and making a reasoned judgement.

6 Evaluate the effectiveness of strategies used to manage urban growth.   [5]

Sample student response	Commentary
Urban growth strategies help cities to grow. Some cities grow by building new housing areas. Urban growth can also cause problems like more traffic. Strategies can work, but sometimes they don't fix all the problems, like pollution.	It isn't clear whether the student understands the strategies to manage urban growth. They talk about building new houses, but they don't evaluate the impact of this as a strategy. They identify some problems of urban growth, but these are not linked to any specific strategy, which means that they haven't really answered the question.

Sample student response	Commentary
Urban growth strategies include things like building new housing, improving public transport and setting aside green spaces. Building new housing areas with efficient transport systems helps to manage growth. In some cities there are problems with air pollution, and more houses lead to overcrowding. Having more green spaces can reduce pollution, but they don't always work in every city. These strategies are effective in controlling urban growth, but they don't fully deal with issues like traffic congestion and pollution.	This response is more detailed. It is clear that the student understands some urban growth strategies as they are able to name some. This response also gives benefits and problems with some of the strategies and has an overall conclusion. The inclusion of case studies would further improve this answer.
Urban growth strategies, such as building new houses, improving public transport and creating green spaces, can all be successful. In Singapore, the development of housing alongside public transport has allowed urban growth to happen without causing too much congestion and pollution. Green spaces can be effective in reducing pollution, but only if combined with other strategies like waste management. In cities like Mumbai, rapid urban growth has not been managed well, which has led to informal settlements and overcrowding. The effectiveness of strategies to manage urban growth depends on the city's specific challenges. A combination of strategies is most effective.	This response is very clear. It evaluates some of the strategies used to manage urban growth, explaining how some work and others do not. It also uses case studies to exemplify the points being made, which improves the overall quality of the answer. The final two sentences provide a good conclusion, which addresses the question well.

Considering the example answers, put what you have learned into practice with the following questions.

7 Evaluate the effectiveness of aid in promoting sustainable development. [5]

8 Evaluate the role of tourism on the economic development of a named country. [5]

9 Evaluate the effectiveness of strategies used to address global food insecurity. [5]

State

In Topic 7, you also practised answering questions using the 'state' command word. You learned that 'state' means to express in clear terms. Remember that these questions require brief and direct answers.

10 State **three** different land uses in the rural-urban fringe shown in Figure 4. [3]

Figure 4

Cambridge IGCSE Geography (0460) Paper 11, Q2a(iii), June 2023

Sample student response	Commentary
pitch, shops	This response correctly identifies a pitch. The student also identifies shops, but there are no shops in the image. This response also only identifies two land uses, when the question asks for three.
I can see a stadium in the main bit of the picture. There is also some leisure places and some woodland all around the edges of the picture.	The response correctly identifies a stadium. They suggest leisure, but this is the same land use as stadium. They also explain where they can see each feature, but explanations aren't necessary for a 'state' question.
stadium, woodland, housing	This response correctly identifies three different land uses from the image.

Considering the example answers, put what you have learned into practice with the following questions.

11 Using Figure 5, state the percentage of air pollution in the USA caused by carbon monoxide. [1]

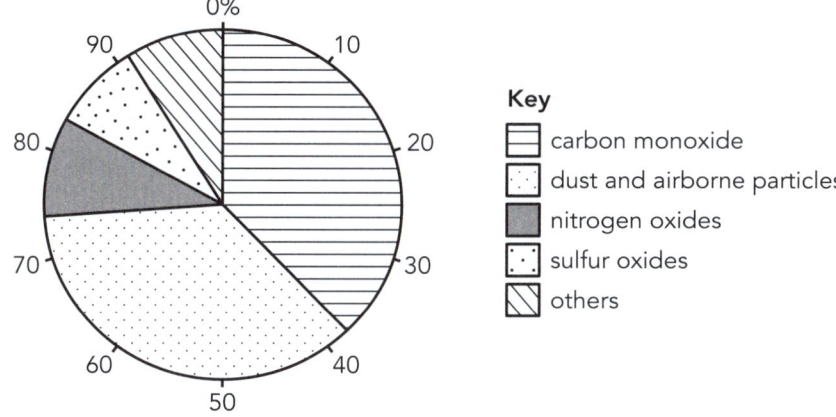

The main types of air pollution in the USA

Key
- carbon monoxide
- dust and airborne particles
- nitrogen oxides
- sulfur oxides
- others

Figure 5

Adapted from Cambridge IGCSE Geography (0460) Paper 12, Q6a(i), June 2024

12 State **one** example of a job in the primary sector. [1]

13 Study Figure 6, which shows information on sources of energy which were used in Japan in 2013 and are planned to be used in 2030.

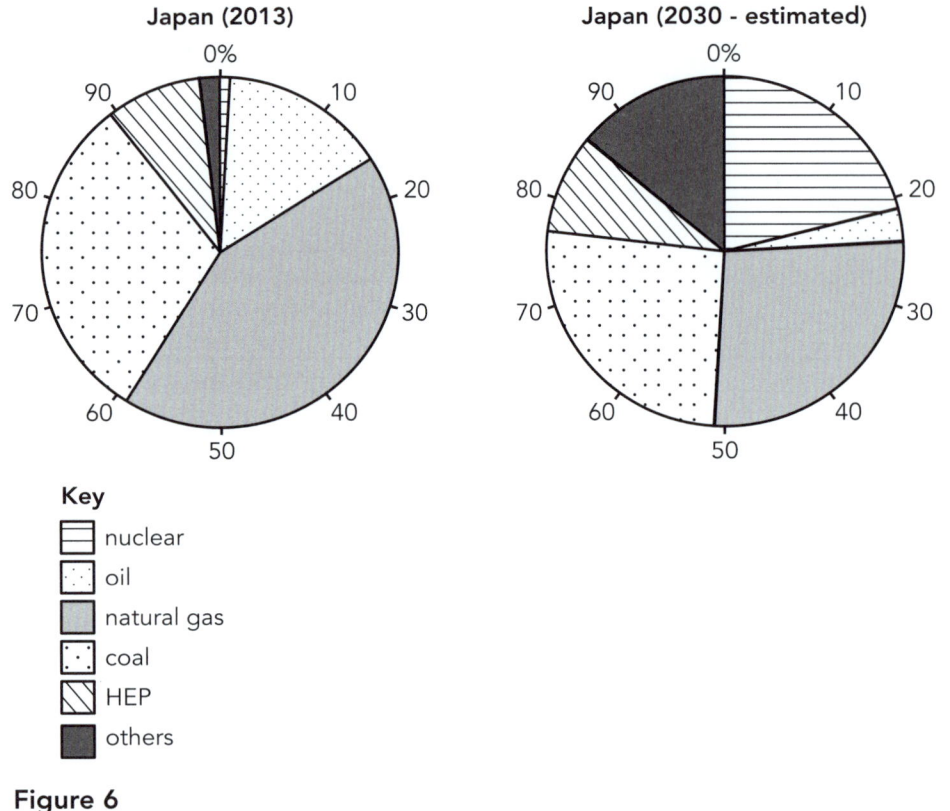

Key

- nuclear
- oil
- natural gas
- coal
- HEP
- others

Figure 6

State **two** pieces of evidence from Figure 6 that Japan plans to reduce the use of fossil fuels by 2030. [2]

Cambridge IGCSE Geography (0460) Paper 13, Q6a(ii), June 2019

Plot

In Topic 8, you reviewed how to approach the 'plot' command word. You learned that 'plot' means to mark point(s) on a graph/diagram/map. Remember, when responding to 'plot' questions, it is essential to place the information clearly and accurately, using the correct scale, symbols or coordinates.

14 Study Figure 7, a graph showing information about air pollution in the USA (an HIC in North America). **Complete Figure 7** by plotting the following information (see PPQ 14 in the Resource Sheets):

- nitrogen oxides: 9%

- sulfur oxides: 8%. [2]

The main types of air pollution in the USA

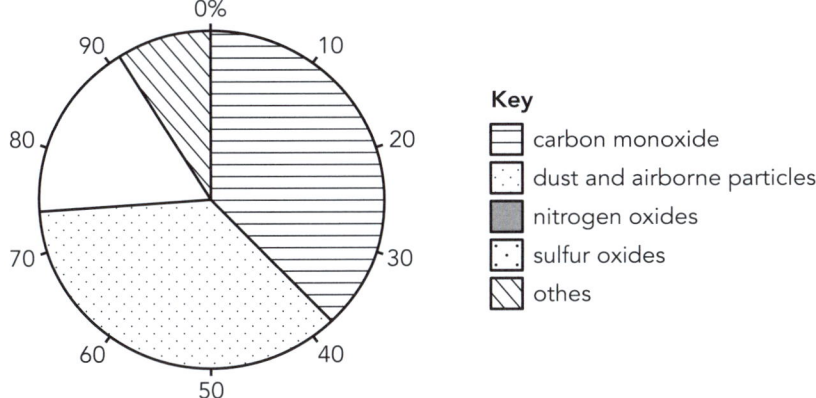

Key
☐ carbon monoxide
☐ dust and airborne particles
☐ nitrogen oxides
☐ sulfur oxides
☐ othes

Figure 7

Adapted from Cambridge IGCSE Geography (0460) Paper 12, Q6a(ii), June 2024

Sample student response	Commentary
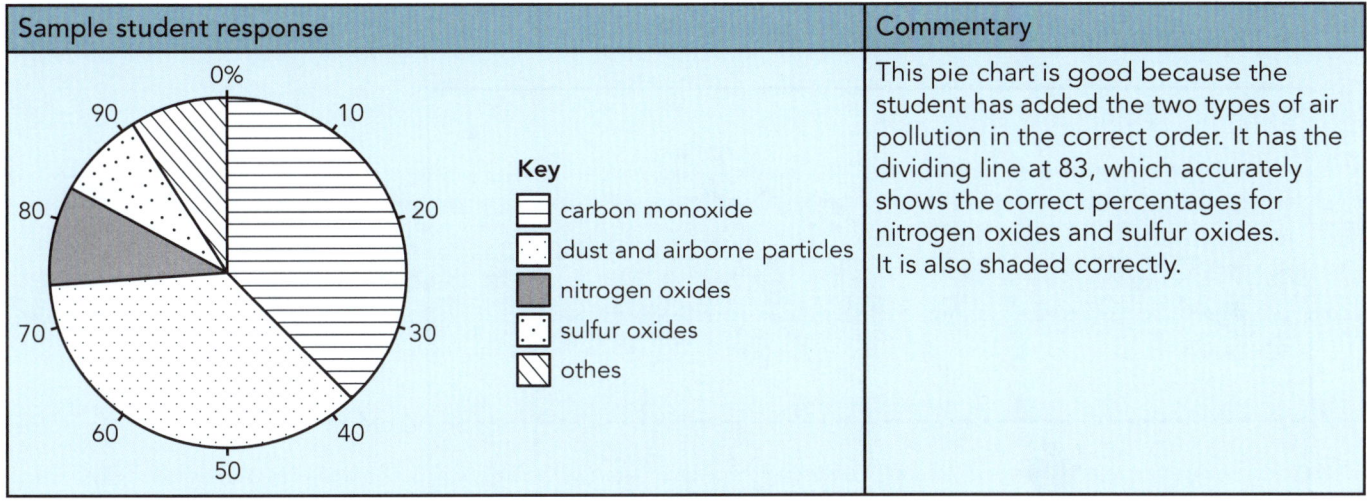	This pie chart is good because the student has added the two types of air pollution in the correct order. It has the dividing line at 83, which accurately shows the correct percentages for nitrogen oxides and sulfur oxides. It is also shaded correctly.

Considering the example answer, put what you have learned into practice with the following questions, making copies of the figures first.

15 Study Figure 8, showing information about migrants from islands in the Pacific Ocean to New Zealand. **Complete Figure 8** by plotting the following information about the origin of migrants from islands in the Pacific Ocean to New Zealand (see PPQ 15 in the Resource Sheets).

Samoa = 43%

Cook Islands = 23%

Tonga = 14%   [3]

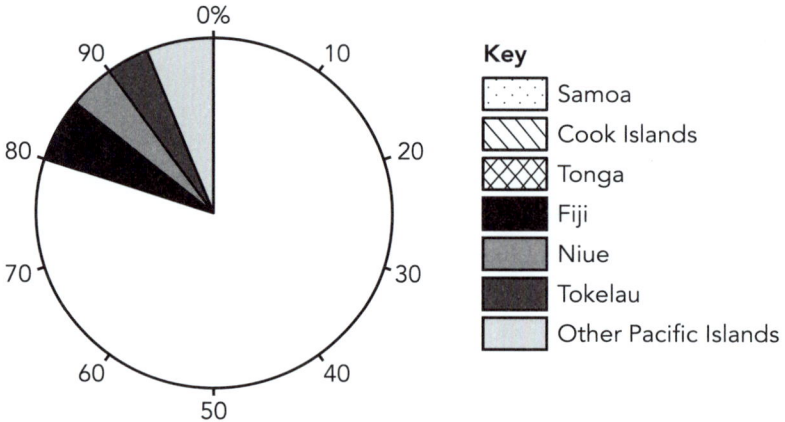

Figure 8

Cambridge IGCSE Geography (0460) Paper 13, Q1b(i), November 2023

16 Study Figure 9, which shows information about population density in Europe in 2018. **Complete Figure 9** by plotting the following information (see PPQ 16 in the Resource Sheets):

The population density of Spain is 91 people per km². [1]

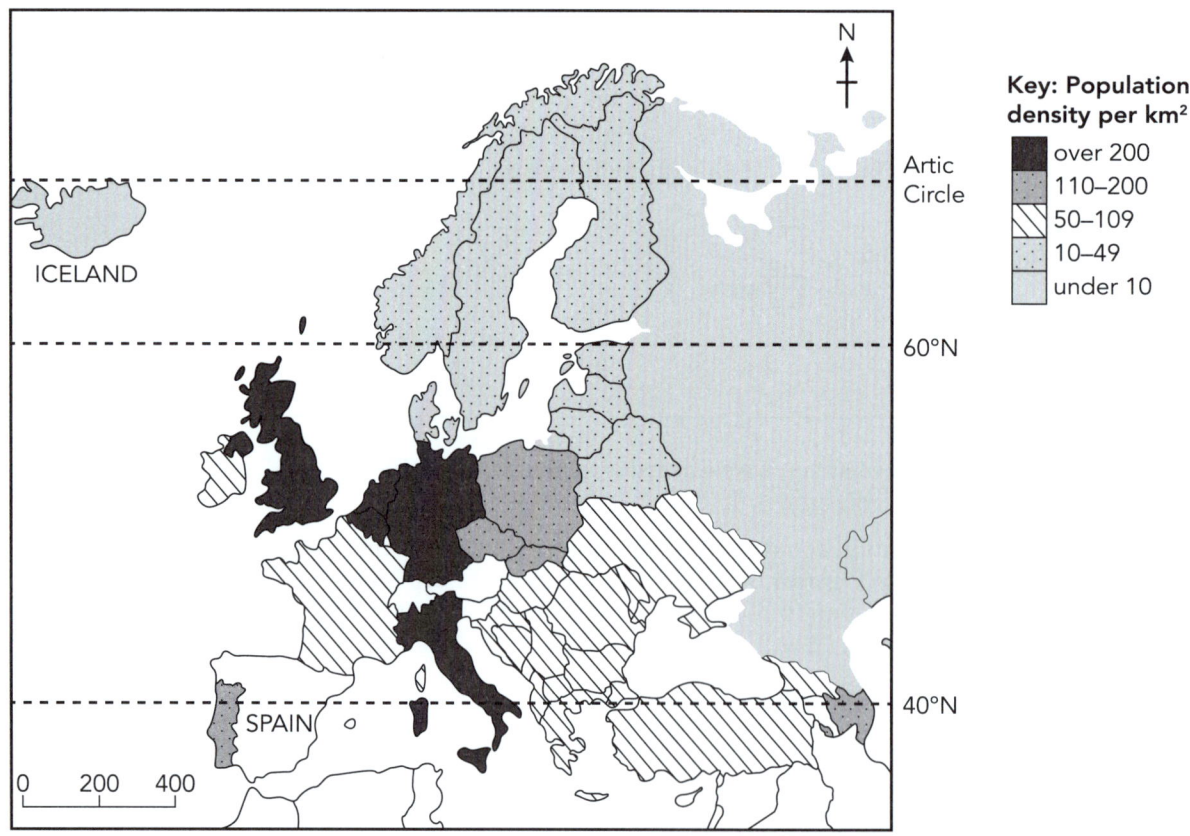

Figure 9

Cambridge IGCSE Geography (0460) Paper 13, Q1a(i), November 2021

17 Study Figure 10, which shows information about precipitation and evaporation in Los Gatos, an area in California, USA (an HIC). **Complete Figure 10** by plotting the following (see PPQ 17 in the Resource Sheets):

The average precipitation in January is 130 mm.   [1]

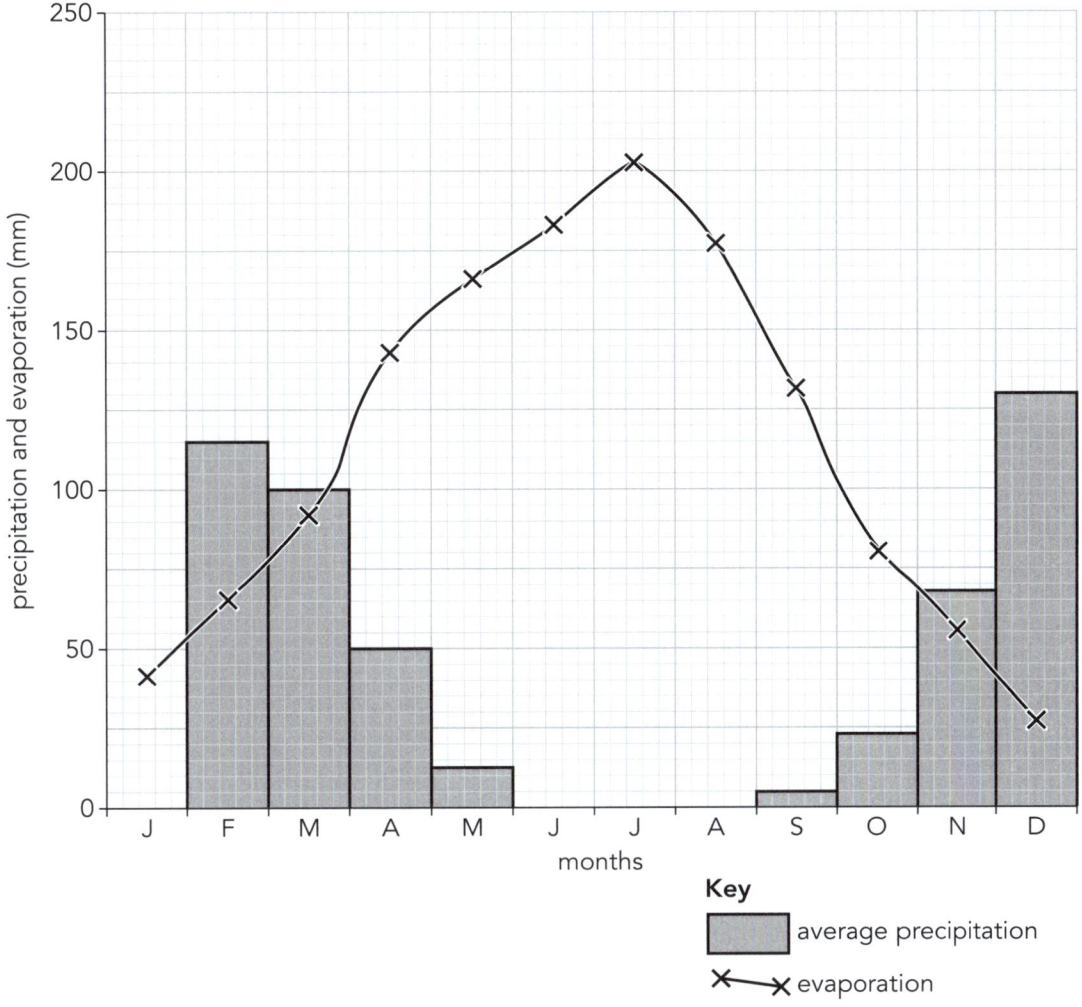

Figure 10

Adapted from Cambridge IGCSE Geography (0460) Paper 12, Q6a(i), June 2021

To what extent

In Topic 8, you also reviewed the assessment phrase 'to what extent'. You learned that 'to what extent' means to assess the degree to which something is true or accurate. Remember that these questions require you to evaluate evidence, analyse information and form a balanced conclusion.

18 Study Figure 11, which is a scatter graph showing the relationship between the Human Development Index (HDI) for a country and the percentage of its population with access to improved water sources.

To what extent is there a relationship between the Human Development Index (HDI) and the percentage of the population with access to improved water sources? You should use statistics to support your answer. [3]

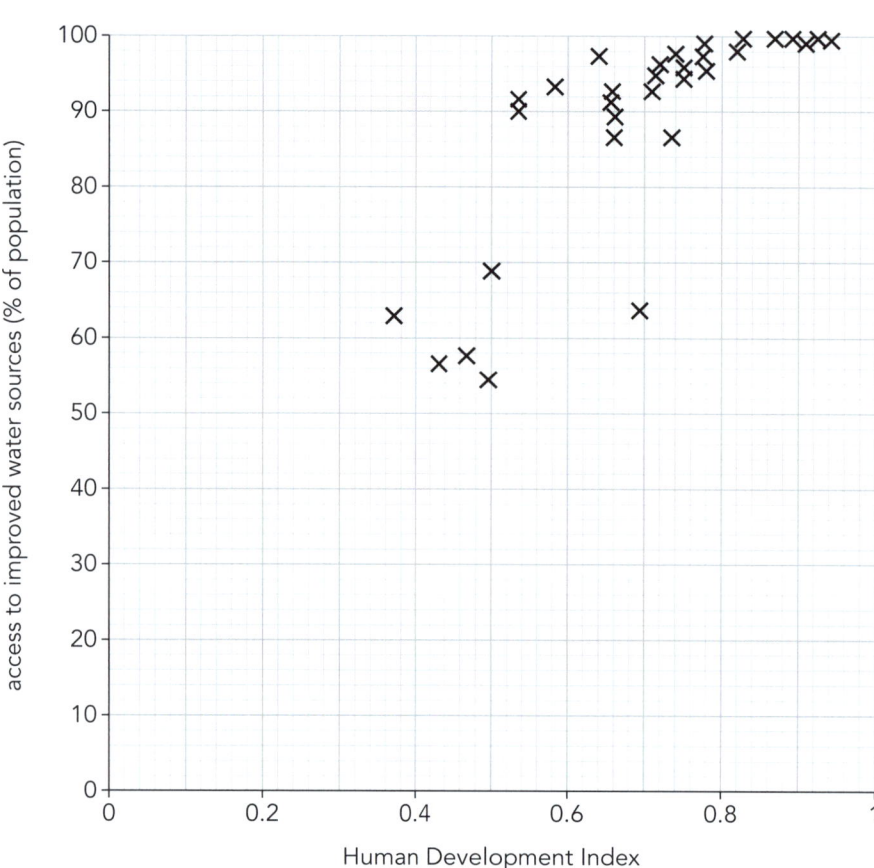

Figure 11

Cambridge IGCSE Geography (0460) Paper 11, Q5b(i), November 2022

Sample student response	Commentary
As HDI increases, the percentage of people with access to water also increases.	The student identifies the relationship between HDI and the percentage of people who have access to water. However, they only make this one point and they do not use any data from the graph, so the response is basic.
There is a positive correlation between HDI and the percentage of people with access to water. However, there are anomalies, for example one country has a high HDI, but relatively low access to water.	This response is more detailed. It identifies the relationship between HDI and the percentage of people who have access to water, and it also recognises that there are anomalies. These are two key points. This answer would have been improved with the use of data from the graph.

Sample student response	Commentary
There is a positive correlation between HDI and the percentage of people with access to water. The population of countries with HDI above 0.5 generally have good access to water sources. There are some anomalies within the relationship, for example one country has an HDI of 0.7, but only has 63% access to water.	This response is detailed. It identifies the relationship between HDI and the percentage of people who have access to water. It also recognises that there are anomalies and it has clear use of data from the graph.

Considering the example answers, put what you have learned into practice with the following questions.

19 Study Figure 12, which shows information about the relationship between two indicators of development in selected countries.

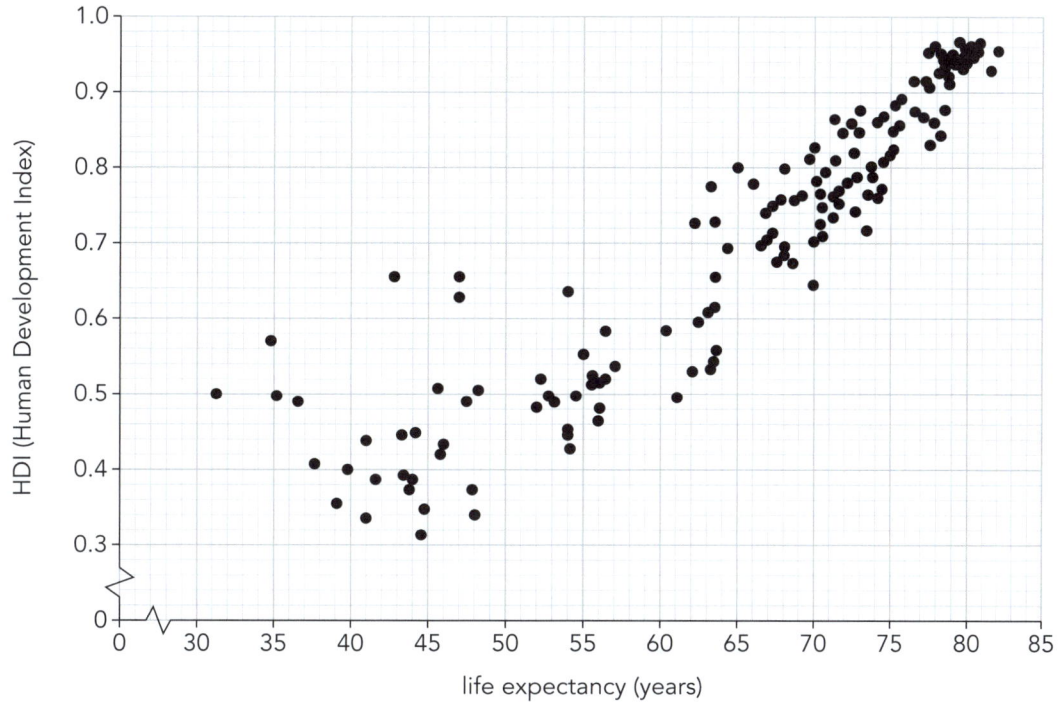

Figure 12

To what extent does Figure 12 show that there is a relationship between HDI and life expectancy? [2]

Cambridge IGCSE Geography (0460) Paper 13, Q6a(ii), November 2021

20 Study Figure 13, a map of Hulhumalé, an island in the Maldives. A new hotel is being built. The new hotel is located at **X** in Figure 13.

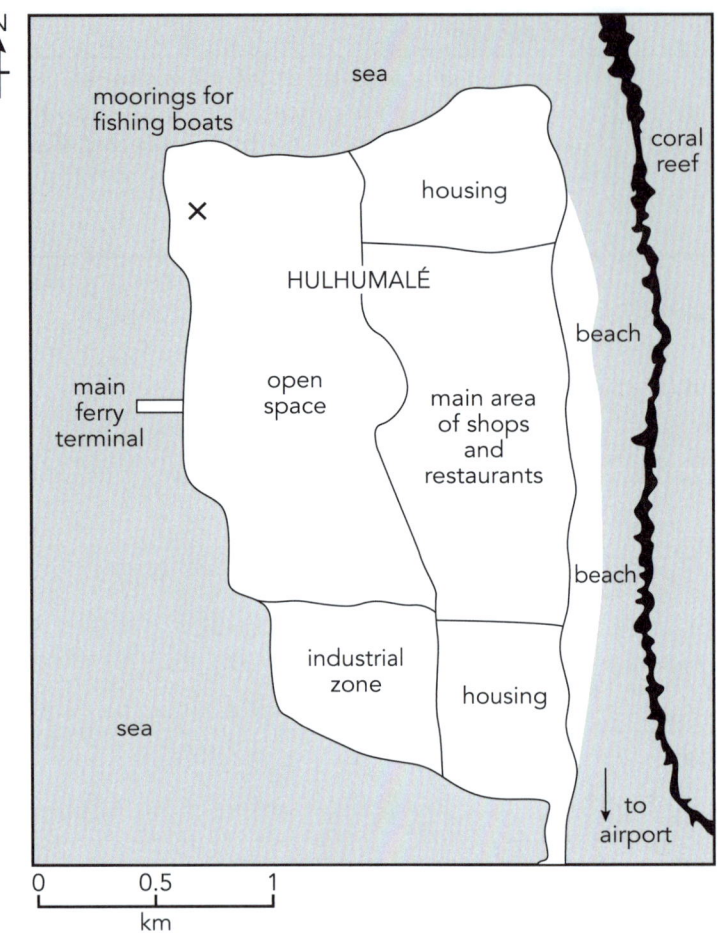

Figure 13

To what extent is **X** an ideal location for a new hotel?
Give reasons for your answer. [3]

Cambridge IGCSE Geography (0460) Paper 11, Q5b(i), November 2020

21 To what extent is food aid an effective long-term solution to food insecurity
in low-income countries? [5]

Locate

In Topic 9, you practised using the 'locate' command word. You learned that 'locate'
means to indicate the position of a place, feature or entity from/in a resource.
The resource could be a map, image or diagram. Remember that locating features
accurately is a key geographical skill, requiring precise identification.

22 Study Figure 14, which shows the movement of Syrian refugees into
neighbouring countries in 2020. Locate the country that hosted the most
refugees from Syria in 2020. [1]

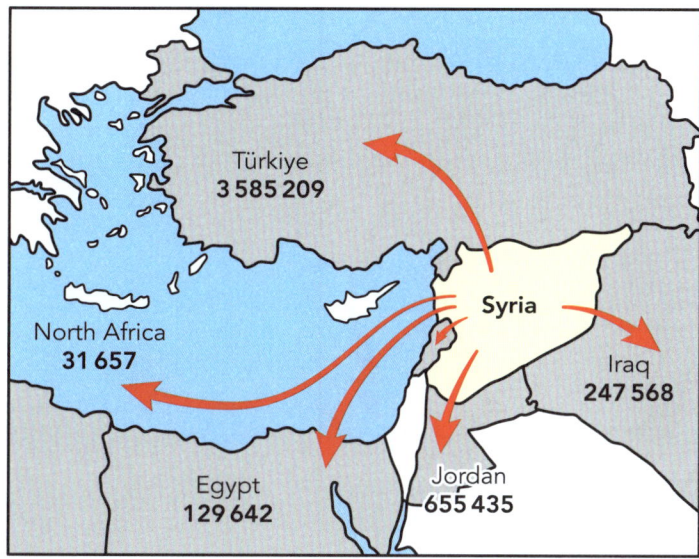

Figure 14

Sample student response	Commentary
Jordan	This is incorrect. Jordan did not receive the highest number of refugees from Syria in 2020.
Europe	This response is also incorrect; it suggests an answer that is not shown on Figure 14, and it names a continent rather than a country.
Türkiye	This response is correct as Figure 14 shows that Türkiye hosted 3 585 209 Syrian refugees in 2020, which is a higher figure than any other country in Figure 14.

Considering the example answers, put what you have learned into practice with the following questions.

23 Figure 15 shows a GIS hazard map of a volcano, Villarrica, in Chile, South America. Locate a settlement that is at high risk from lahars and lava flows. [1]

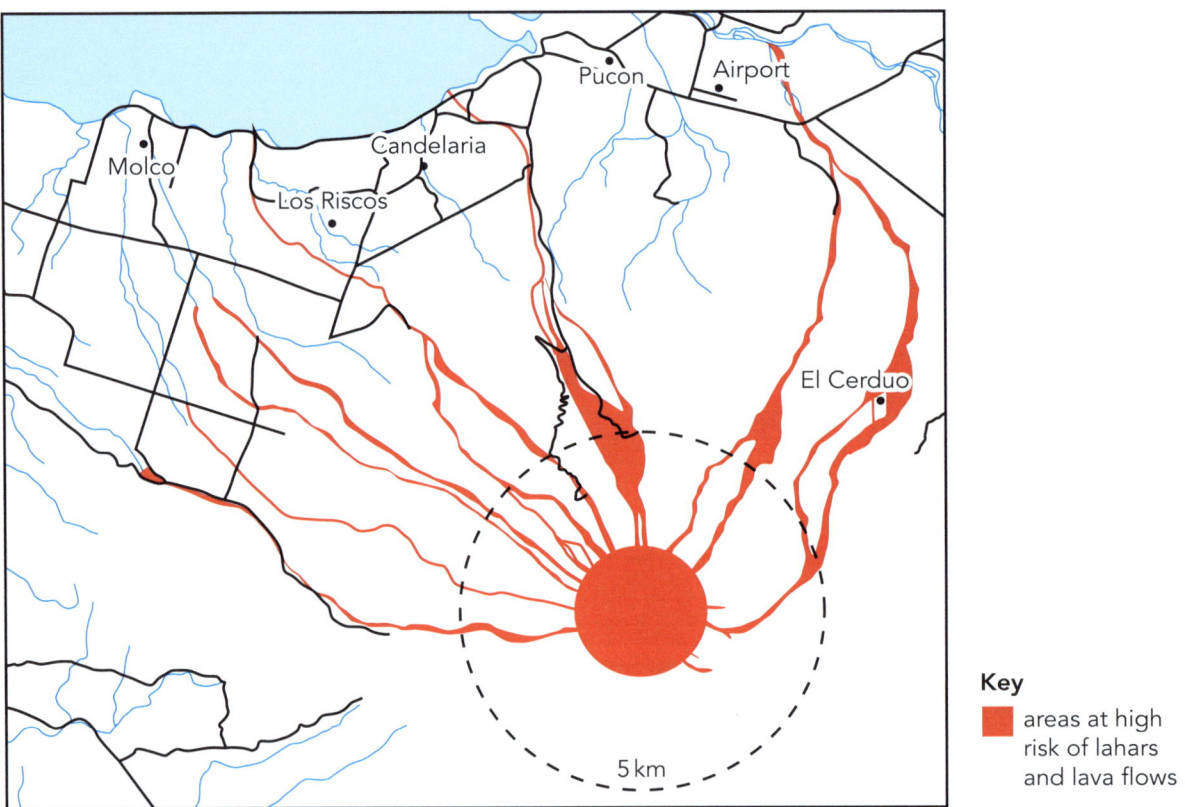

Figure 15

24 Study Figure 16, which shows the income groups of countries. Locate the continent that has the most low-income and lower-middle-income countries. [1]

■ Low-income ■ Lower-middle income ■ Upper-middle income ■ High-income

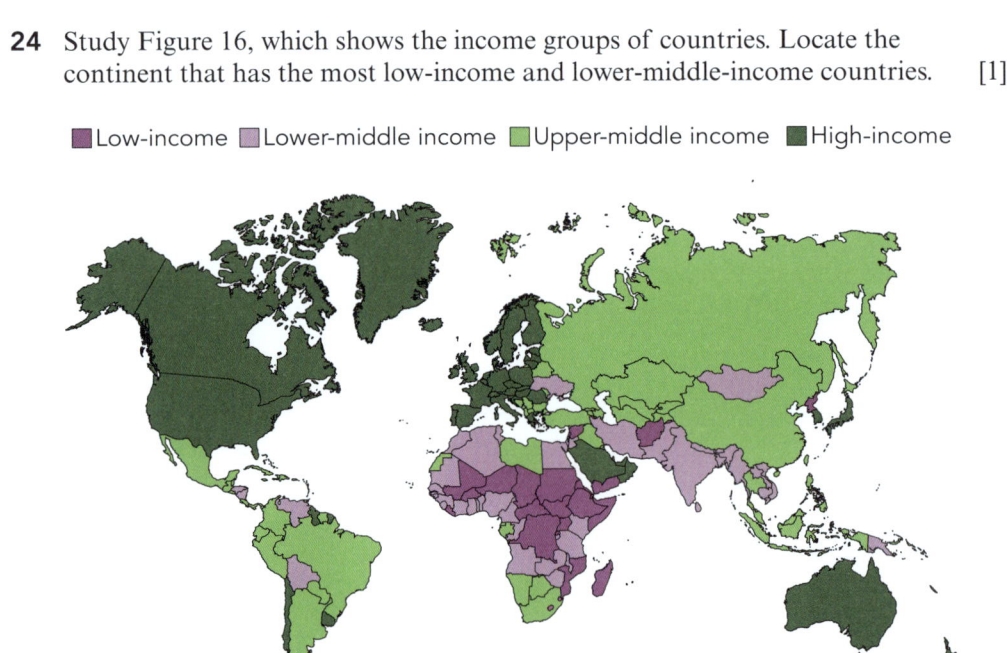

Figure 16

25 Figure 17 shows the daily supply of calories per person for different countries globally in 2018. Locate a country where the daily supply of calories per person is 3800 kcals or above. [1]

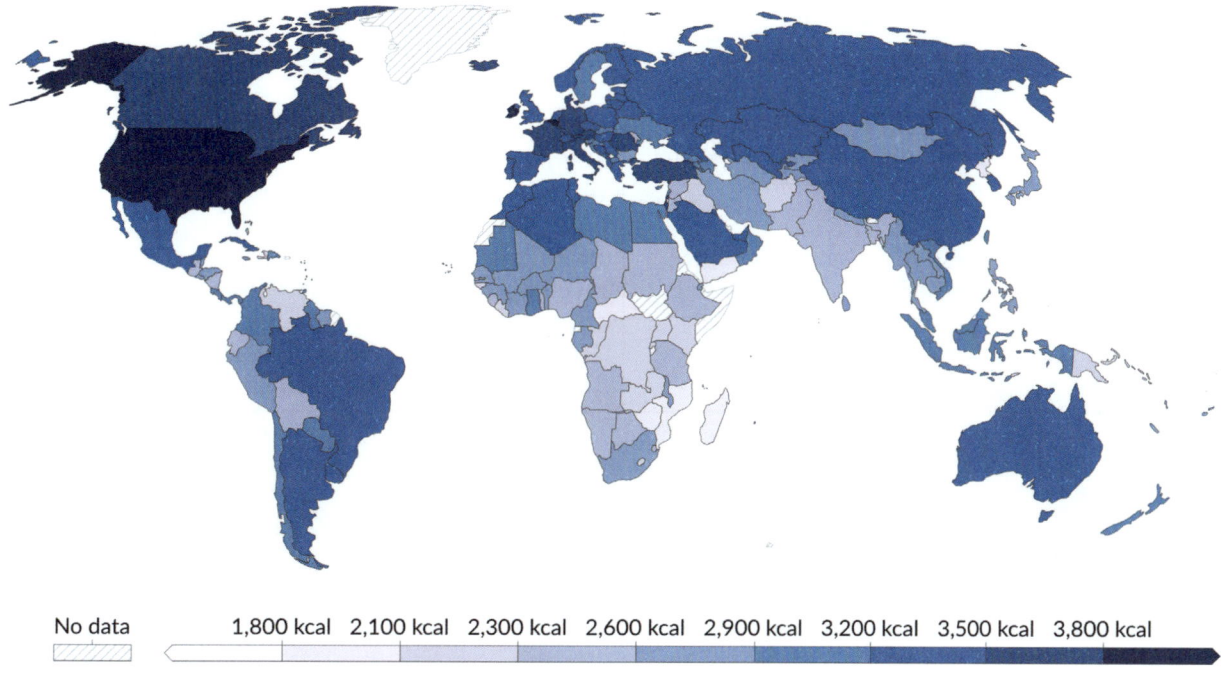

No data   1,800 kcal   2,100 kcal   2,300 kcal   2,600 kcal   2,900 kcal   3,200 kcal   3,500 kcal   3,800 kcal

Figure 17

How far do you agree

In Topic 9, you also reviewed the assessment phrase 'how far do you agree'. You learned that 'how far' means you do not have to fully agree or disagree with a statement, but instead you can agree or disagree to some extent. Remember that this type of question requires you to consider both sides of an issue, weigh the evidence, and make a judgement based on that analysis.

26 How far do you agree that the challenges of urbanisation outweigh its benefits in low-income countries? [7]

Sample student response	Commentary
I agree that the challenges of urbanisation in low-income countries outweigh its benefits. One of the main challenges is the rapid population growth in cities, which results in overcrowded living conditions. In some cities, a large percentage of the population lives in informal settlements with poor sanitation and inadequate access to clean water. This leads to the spread of diseases. The rise in demand for jobs causes high levels of unemployment, leaving many people without an income, which leads to poverty. Urbanisation also has benefits. Cities provide more jobs and access to services. Urbanisation can also lead to the development of better roads and healthcare facilities. These things can improve the quality of life for people. While urbanisation brings some benefits, I believe the challenges outweigh the benefits.	This answer is structured into paragraphs, which makes it easy to read. The first paragraph talks about challenges and the second paragraph talks about benefits. The student has also made it clear whether they agree with the statement, so they have answered the question well. The student could have also added depth and balance to their answer by giving detail about their ideas in paragraph two. There are also no case studies in this answer. Including case studies can strengthen the argument being made. For example, Dhaka in Bangladesh would have fit into paragraph one, where they discuss informal settlements, and Lagos in Nigeria would have fit into paragraph two, where they discuss jobs and infrastructure.

Considering the example answer, put what you have learned into practice with the following questions.

27 How far do you agree that foreign aid is essential for the development of low-income countries? [7]

28 How far do you agree that globalisation has only benefitted high-income countries? [7]

29 How far do you agree that solar power is the best renewable energy source for generating electricity worldwide? [7]

Give

In Topic 10, you practised using the command word 'give'. You learned that 'give' means to produce an answer from a given source or recall/memory.

Considering the example answers, put what you have learned into practice with the following questions.

30 Study Figure 19, which shows four plans which the government of an HIC in Europe is considering to maintain energy supplies in the future.

Plan 1
Build a new nuclear power station.
Plan 2
Increase the amount of wind generators offshore and in the mountains.
Plan 3
Search for oil and gas in offshore areas.
Plan 4
Import large amounts of coal from China.

Figure 19

Give **three** reasons why some people in the country may object to Plan 1. [3]

Adapted from Cambridge IGCSE Geography (0460) Paper 11, Q6b(i), June 2023

31 Give **one** example of jobs in each of the following:

- tertiary sector

- quaternary sector [2]

Cambridge IGCSE Geography (0460) Paper 11, Q5a(ii), November 2022

32 Give **two** reasons for falling death rates in Stage 2 of the Demographic Transition Model, shown in Figure 20. [2]

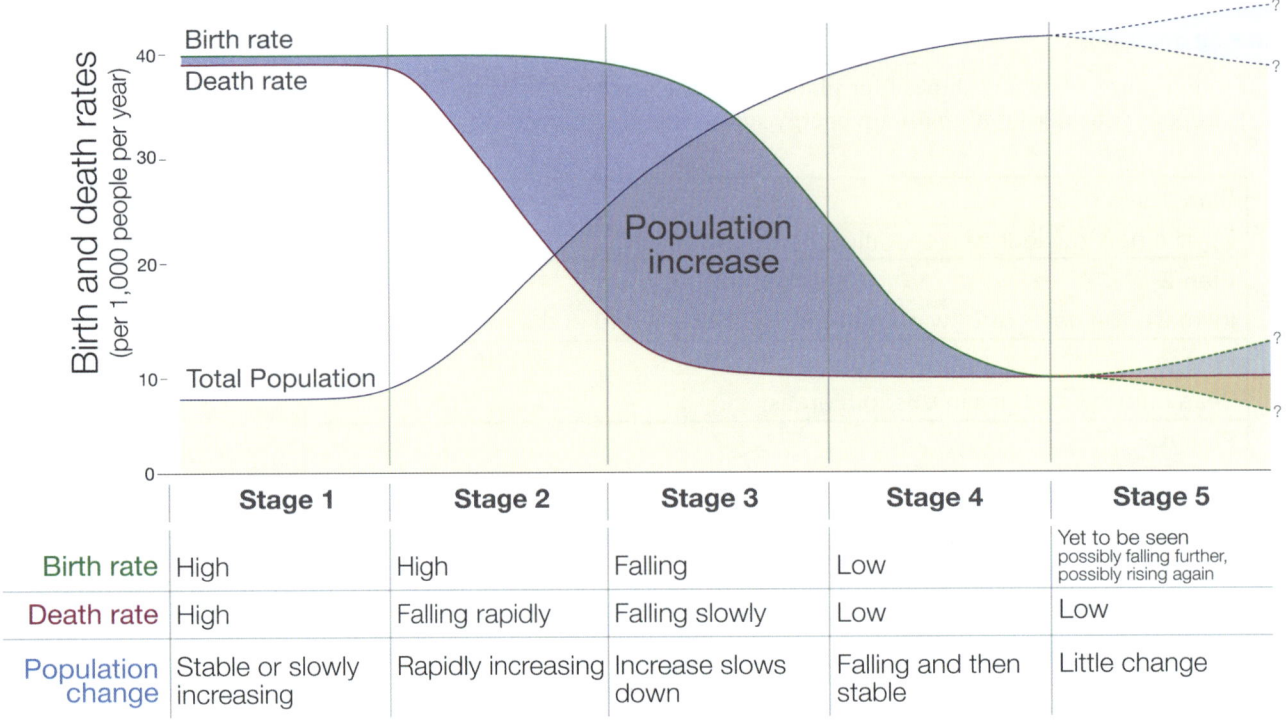

Figure 20

Justify

You also reviewed how to approach the command word 'justify' in Topic 10. You learned that 'justify' means to support an answer with evidence.

33 Study Figure 21, which is a table showing information about GDP per person, access to improved water sources and life expectancy in five MICs/LICs.

GDP per person is a measure of wealth.

	GDP per person (US $)	Access to improved water sources (%)	Life expectancy (years)
Mexico	18 900	96	76
Paraguay	9400	98	77
Philippines	7700	92	69
Thailand	16 800	98	75
Venezuela	15 100	93	76

Figure 21

Which country, listed in Figure 21, has the lowest level of development? Justify your answer. [3]

Adapted from Cambridge IGCSE Geography (0460) Paper 11, Q5b(i), November 2019

Sample student response	Commentary
Country: Thailand Justification: Thailand has a lower GDP per person than Mexico. However, it has a higher percentage of people with access to clean water than the Philippines. Life expectancy in Thailand is also quite good. Therefore, I believe it has a good level of development compared to the others.	The response is incorrect because it does not directly address the question, which asks for the country with the lowest level of development. The student wrongly selects Thailand instead of the Philippines, which is the correct country. The student's justification is based on comparing countries in a general way without focusing on the specific countries mentioned in the table.
Country: Philippines Justification: The Philippines has the lowest GDP per person, at $7700, which shows it is the poorest country in terms of wealth. It also has the lowest access to clean water at 92%, and its life expectancy of 69 years is the lowest compared to the others.	The response is okay, but there is room for improvement. The student correctly selects the Philippines as the country with the lowest level of development. However, the justification could be more precise in linking all the factors (GDP; water access; life expectancy) to the idea of development and why the Philippines ranks the lowest.
Country: Philippines Justification: The Philippines has the lowest GDP per person at $7700, which indicates it is the least wealthy country. It also has the lowest life expectancy at 69 years, meaning people in the country tend to live shorter lives. Its access to clean water is only 92%, which is the lowest of the countries listed. These factors combined show that the Philippines has the lowest level of development.	This response is excellent. It directly addresses the question, provides a clear and accurate justification and links the key indicators of development to the country's level of development. The student explains the significance of each factor in a way that is easy to understand.

Now write an improved answer to Question 34.

Geographical Enquiry

Geographical enquiry

KNOWLEDGE FOCUS

You will answer questions on:

- 11.1 Understanding the route to geographical enquiry and planning fieldwork
- 11.2 Data collection methods, fieldwork safety and equipment
- 11.3 Presenting and analysing data
- 11.4 Making conclusions

EXAM SKILLS FOCUS

In this topic you will:

- show that you understand the command word 'devise' and answer a 'devise' question
- show that you understand the command word 'estimate' and answer an 'estimate' question
- show that you understand the command word 'suggest' and answer a 'suggest' question.

The route to geographical enquiry is assessed through Component 3, Coursework or Paper 4, Geographical Investigations. Both options have an emphasis on testing Assessment Objective 2 Skills and analysis, but also have elements of Assessment Objective 1 Knowledge and understanding, and Assessment Objective 3 Evaluation and decision-making. Paper 4 contains two compulsory questions, each of which are worth 30 marks. The questions can relate to topics covered in Paper 1 or 2.

The command word 'devise' means to create a questionnaire to present other information according to specific requirements. When answering 'devise' questions, make sure that your questionnaire is clear and meets the requirements of the question.

The command word 'estimate' means to use judgement to give a unit value to a distance or area. When answering 'estimate' questions, it is important to use any scales, measurements or references that are provided.

'Suggest' means to apply knowledge and understanding to situations where there are a range of valid responses in order to make proposals/put forward considerations. Unlike questions with fixed answers, 'suggest' questions test your ability to think logically, make predictions and consider different geographical factors. You practised 'suggest' questions in Topic 4 – this unit offers another chance to apply your understanding of this command word, but to enquiry-based questions.

11.1 Understanding the route to geographical enquiry and planning fieldwork

1   Put the following in order to show the steps to completing fieldwork:

   • analyse results

   • collect data

   • decide what data to collect and how to collect it

   • check results against hypothesis

   • make conclusions

   • form a hypothesis

   • present results

2   Sort the following statements about setting an aim and formulating hypotheses into 'true' or 'false':

   • the aim should be simple

   • the aim should be complex

   • the aim should identify many questions

   • the aim should identify one question

   • a hypothesis is a prediction

   • hypotheses are always proven to be correct

3   Copy the following text and complete by choosing the correct word in the brackets.

   Near the (**end/start**) of your fieldwork project, you should check if the data supports your hypothesis. The information you collect will prove, partially prove or (**support/disprove**) your hypothesis. If your data does not support your hypothesis, you start again, (**resetting/repeating**) a hypothesis and retesting.

When estimating, it is important to apply any scales, measurements or reference points the questions give you. Your answers to 'estimate' questions should be based on clear evidence and logical reasoning, rather than random guesses.

Questions that use the command word 'suggest' require you to apply your knowledge – remember that there is not one fixed answer, so you will have to use logical thinking.

4 A student has collected the data in Table 11.1 for a river study fieldwork:

Site	Depth of the river (cm)
A	5
B	6
C	7
D	12
E	15

Table 11.1: Data for a river study fieldwork

Estimate the average depth of the river. Choose the closest estimate from the list below:

a 4 cm

b 6 cm

c 9 cm

d 14 cm   [1]

5 A geography class is planning to investigate the number of people using a local park at different times of the day. Suggest a way to record and present this data.   [4]

6 A student is carrying out research into waste collection services in different parts of a city in a low-income country (LIC). Their data can be found in Table 11.2.

Area	Waste collection service?
A	Yes
B	Yes
C	No
D	Yes
E	No

Table 11.2: Data about waste collection services in different parts of a city

Estimate the percentage of the city that has access to a waste collection service. Choose the closest estimate from the list below:

a 20%

b 40%

c 60%

d 80%   [1]

« RECALL AND CONNECT 1 «

Fieldwork can be carried out to test models and theories about rivers. One example is the Bradshaw model. See if you can answer these questions about the Bradshaw model linked to Topic 1, 'Rivers'.

a What is the Bradshaw model?

b According to the Bradshaw model, how does discharge change from upstream to downstream?

c According to the Bradshaw model, which river characteristics or features decrease from upstream to downstream?

UNDERSTAND THIS TERM

- Hypothesis

REFLECTION

You must plan and carry out fieldwork in a particular order – this is known as the route to geographical enquiry. Remembering the order is easier if you understand the process. For example, you cannot collect data until you have decided which methods of data collection to use. Creating a flow chart often helps to understand a process. Can you create a flow chart to show how you can plan and carry out fieldwork? How many stages would it have? What would each stage be?

7 Match the following terms, a–e, to their correct definition or example of the term, 1–5.

a	Hypothesis	1	Formed from a question that will be analysed using data.
b	Investigator bias	2	A statement that can be tested.
c	A statement that can be tested	3	A student only asking their friends in their class questions in a mobile phone survey.
d	Evaluation of a hypothesis	4	Choosing data that influences the outcome of a study.
e	Example of bias	5	Using collected data to determine if the hypothesis was true or false.

8 What makes a good hypothesis?

9 How does investigator bias affect research outcomes?

When devising a questionnaire, you need to ensure that your questions are relevant and clearly worded. This means avoiding unnecessary or vague questions and producing a questionnaire that is well-structured.

10 A student is investigating whether a local town has enough leisure facilities. Devise a questionnaire question that they could ask. [1]

11 A student is investigating whether locals are happy with the number of tourists visiting their coastal town. Devise a questionnaire question that they could ask.   [1]

12 A fieldwork group wants to test the hypothesis: 'People prefer to use public transport rather than private cars in city centres.' Devise a questionnaire question that they could ask to test this hypothesis.   [1]

REFLECTION

A good hypothesis is simple and testable. Can you think of a hypothesis that can be created about coastal erosion? How would you devise an overall aim or question for an investigation about coastal erosion, and how would you then turn this into a hypothesis?

11.2 Data collection methods, fieldwork safety and equipment

1 a Match the following types of questions found on questionnaires, a–c, to their definitions, 1–3.

a	multiple-choice	1	longer, and more unique, answers can be given
b	closed	2	respondents have a choice of answers
c	open	3	answers are limited, e.g. 'yes' or 'no'

   b Write an example question to match each question type.

2 Decide if the following statements are true or false. If they are false, correct them:

   a An enquiry checklist only needs to include primary data collection methods.

   b Closed questions allow respondents to give longer, opinion-based answers.

   c A pilot study can help avoid issues with question clarity.

   d Interviews are less expensive and faster to conduct than questionnaires.

   e Questionnaires can be done face-to-face, online or over the phone.

3 Read the following scenario and then answer Questions a to c below:

   A team of geography students is preparing a field trip to investigate the impact of tourism in a coastal town. They plan to use questionnaires to gather data from tourists and interviews with local shop owners.

   a Identify three preparations the students should include in their fieldwork checklist.

b What are the potential challenges of using questionnaires with tourists, and how can they address these challenges?

c Suggest one advantage and one disadvantage of interviewing local shop owners compared to using questionnaires with tourists.

4 What is the difference between:

a random sampling and systematic sampling?

b primary and secondary data?

5 A student is investigating how people feel about new sea defences that have been put in place along the coastline. Devise two relevant questions that could be included in a questionnaire. [2]

6 A fieldwork group wants to investigate the width and depth of a river at several points along its course. Suggest a method to accurately measure these characteristics. [4]

7 Copy the following text and complete by choosing the correct word in the brackets.

Taking part in fieldwork poses risks and (**hazards/questions**) that need to be identified before the investigation starts. To ensure clear and effective communication, always share (**location/contact**) details and work in pairs or groups. Environmental conditions to consider include (**dressing/walking**) appropriately, using (**sunblock/resources**), and avoiding dangerous areas.

8 Read the following scenario and answer Questions a to c below: A group of students is conducting fieldwork near a river. They are collecting data using transects and taking photographs. They notice the riverbank is steep, and one student has a bee allergy.

a Identify three potential risks in this scenario.

b Suggest three ways the group can address these risks to ensure safety during their fieldwork.

c What additional equipment or preparation might be needed for this location?

9 Read the following scenario and answer Questions a to d below: A team of students is conducting fieldwork in a forested area to survey plant biodiversity. They are using quadrats to collect data and they are taking field sketches. The area is isolated with uneven terrain, some parts are muddy, and there are reports of ticks in the area.

a Identify three potential risks in this scenario.

b Suggest three ways the group can address these risks to ensure safety during their fieldwork.

c How might the students in this scenario use quadrats?

d What additional equipment or preparation might be needed for this location?

10 Suggest a checklist to ensure safety during a fieldwork study taking place in a city centre. [4]

11 A geography teacher is planning a fieldwork trip to study coastal erosion. Suggest three safety measures that should be considered before the trip. [3]

UNDERSTAND THESE TERMS

- Pilot study
- Random sampling
- Systematic sampling
- Primary data
- Secondary data

« RECALL AND CONNECT 2 «

Sand dune ecosystems are located along coastlines. The density and diversity of plant species within sand dunes increase with distance from the shoreline. These two variables can be measured using a quadrat, which is a square that can be placed over short vegetation, making it easier to quantify and identify species. See if you can answer the following questions about sand dune ecosystems linked to Topic 2, 'Coastal environments'.

a Are sand dunes landforms of erosion or deposition?

b Are sand dunes formed by waves or the wind?

- Quadrat

11.3 Presenting and analysing data

1 What is the difference between bar graphs, divided bar graphs and histograms?

2 Decide if the following statements are true or false. If they are false, correct them:

    a Pie charts show data as percentages.

    b Only one line can appear on a line graph.

    c Climate graphs are an example of a combined graph.

    d Scatter graphs can also be called dispersion graphs.

    e Doughnut graphs use symbols to represent each category of data.

    f Triangular graphs represent the relationship between two variables.

    g Radial graphs can be useful for showing outliers.

3 Copy the following text and complete by choosing the correct word in the brackets.

When interpreting graphs, it is important to read all information given, such as axes labels, (**titles/samples**) and the units used. You should look for data that is unusual, such as (**highs/gaps**) and (**errors/lows**) and determine if there is a trend – this will help you to decide whether the data agrees or disagrees with the hypothesis and reach a (**method/conclusion**).

4 Students are collecting data about rates of erosion along a stretch of coastline. Suggest a suitable technique that they could use to present this data. [1]

5 A group of students have visited a local mine to identify how industry impacts the local environment. They have collected qualitative data in the form of words. Suggest how they could present this data. [1]

6 A class have been researching how many people in their local town work in the primary, secondary and tertiary sector. Suggest a suitable way to present this data. [1]

- Categorical data
- Outlier
- Quantitative data
- Trend

11.4 Making conclusions

1   Put the following in order to show the steps taken to form a conclusion:

- Use data clearly to support your argument.

- Write a clear statement about the data that supports how strongly the hypothesis was found to be either true or false.

- Acknowledge any unusual results and if possible, explain the reason for them.

- Revisit the hypothesis to determine what you were testing.

2   Read the following scenario and answer Questions a to e below:

A group of geography students conducted fieldwork in a city centre to investigate the relationship between pedestrian footfall and proximity to public transport hubs. They used a combination of pedestrian counts, questionnaires and mapping to collect their data.

The data they collected included:

Pedestrian counts at three locations (A, B and C):

- Location A (next to the main train station): 350 people/hour

- Location B (500 m from the train station): 220 people/hour

- Location C (1 km from the train station): 120 people/hour

Questionnaire results:

- 80% of respondents near Location A said they used public transport to access the city centre.

- 50% of respondents near Location B used public transport.

- 30% of respondents near Location C used public transport.

a   What patterns can be observed in the pedestrian count data?

b   What patterns can be observed in the questionnaire results?

c   Based on the data provided, suggest one possible conclusion about the relationship between the pedestrian count and proximity to public transport hubs.

d   Identify one limitation of the data collection methods used in this study.

e   Suggest an additional data collection method that could strengthen the students' conclusions.

3 A student is measuring the velocity of a river using a float method. Their results are shown in Table 11.3.

Site	Velocity (m/s)
1	0.2
2	0.3
3	0.5
4	0.6
5	0.8

Table 11.3: River velocity at five different sites

Estimate how long it would take for the float to travel 1 metre at Site 3. Choose the closest estimate from the options below:

a 0.5 seconds

b 1 second

c 2 seconds

d 5 seconds [1]

4 A student found the following hypothesis to be true: 'Beach material gets larger towards the top of the beach.' Their results can be found in Table 11.4 below.

Site	Size of beach material (mm)
1 (close to cliff)	40
2	32
3	–
4	14
5 (close to sea)	8

Table 11.4: Beach material size at five different sites

Estimate the size of beach material at Site 3 from the options listed:

a 37 mm

b 22 mm

c 9 mm

d 7 mm [1]

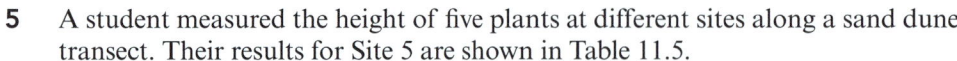
5   A student measured the height of five plants at different sites along a sand dune transect. Their results for Site 5 are shown in Table 11.5.

Plant number	Height (cm)
1	10
2	13
3	11
4	14
5	12

Table 11.5: Plant heights at Site 5

Estimate the average plant height at this site. Choose from:

a   10 cm

b   12 cm

c   14 cm

d   16 cm   [1]

SELF-ASSESSMENT CHECKLIST

Let's revisit the knowledge focus and exam skills focus for this topic.
Decide how confident you are with each statement.

Now I can	Show it	Needs more work	Almost there	Confident to move on
Describe the steps taken in the route to geographical enquiry	What steps must be taken when carrying out a geographical enquiry, and what order do they go in?			
Form hypotheses	What makes a good hypothesis, and can you write one?			
Decide on suitable data collection techniques	How many data collection techniques can you name?			
Plan how to stay safe whilst out in the field	List some risks that could be encountered when carrying out fieldwork and suggest how to limit them.			
Present and analyse data using a suitable technique	List some techniques used to present and analyse quantitative and qualitative data.			

CONTINUED

Now I can	Show it	Needs more work	Almost there	Confident to move on
Make accurate conclusions	What steps must be taken when making conclusions?			
Understand the command word 'devise'	What things need to be considered when devising a questionnaire?			
Understand the command word 'estimate'	Which feature of a map allows you to estimate distance or area?			
Understand the command word 'suggest'	Suggest a method to collect data about the width and depth of a local river.			

Exam practice 3

This section contains both past paper questions and practice questions covering a range of command words found in Paper 4: Geographical Investigations. You will find past paper questions or practice questions following the route to geographical enquiry, with example student responses and commentary. You will then answer similar practice questions or past paper questions. The questions draw together your knowledge and understanding of the route to geographical enquiry and will help you prepare for your assessment.

Understanding the route to geographical enquiry and planning fieldwork

When completing fieldwork, there are several steps you need to take to ensure that your investigation is reliable and unbiased. These steps must be followed in order and are part of the route to geographical enquiry, otherwise known as the scientific method.

Geographical enquiries begin with the formulation of hypotheses – statements that you will set out to accept, partly accept or reject. The following question tests your knowledge about forming hypotheses. It has an example student response and commentary provided. Work through the question first, then compare your answer to the example student response and commentary.

1   A group of students in Thailand studied how the characteristics of a river change downstream. The characteristics are shown in Figure 1.

How the characteristics of a river change downstream

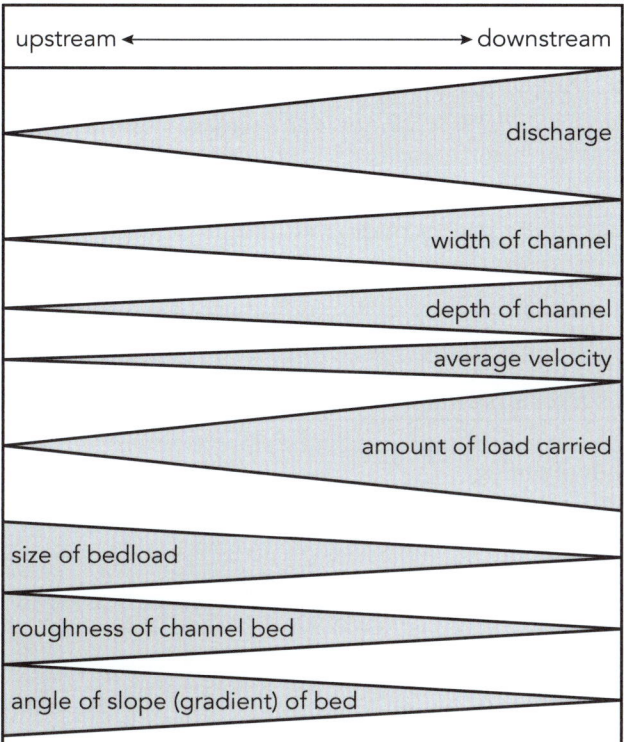

Figure 1

The students decided to investigate two characteristics by testing the following hypotheses at five sites along the River Huai Kup Kap:

Hypothesis 1: Pebbles on the riverbed (bedload) become smaller further downstream.

Hypothesis 2: The angle of slope (gradient) of the riverbed becomes less steep further downstream.

a   Suggest a suitable hypothesis to investigate **one** other characteristic shown in the diagram. Do **not** choose size of bedload or angle of slope (gradient) of the riverbed. [1]

Cambridge IGCSE Geography (0460) Paper 41, Q2e(i), June 2023

Sample student response	Commentary
How wide the river is in different places.	This answer is incorrect as it is not phrased as a hypothesis. A hypothesis needs to be a testable statement, which makes a clear prediction about how a variable changes, for example: 'The width of the river increases further downstream.'
The size of bedload decreases downstream.	The question asked for a hypothesis that was not about the size of bedload or angle of slope. This answer is incorrect as the suggested hypothesis is about the size of bedload.
The channel width increases with distance downstream.	This is a suitable hypothesis as it accurately selects and uses information from Figure 1 and is phrased as a testable statement.

Now try some more questions which test your knowledge about planning fieldwork and understanding the route to geographical enquiry, including Part b of Question 1 above.

b Describe a method to investigate your hypothesis at the five fieldwork sites. [4]

Cambridge IGCSE Geography (0460) Paper 41, Q2e(ii), June 2023

c Before they began their work, the students did a pilot study at a site on the river.

Identify **two** advantages of doing a pilot study from Table 1. Tick (✓) **two** choices. [2]

	Tick (✓)
draw a field sketch of the river's course	
get to know other students before they begin fieldwork	
learn how to work safely in the river	
practise fieldwork techniques	
look at different features along the river	

Table 1

Cambridge IGCSE Geography (0460) Paper 41, Q2a, June 2023

d To investigate **Hypothesis 1:** Pebbles on the riverbed (bedload) become smaller further downstream, the students selected 20 pebbles from the bed of the river at each site.

Which piece of fieldwork equipment from Table 2 did the students use when they measured the length of each pebble? Tick (✓) your choice. [1]

Equipment	Tick (✓)
callipers	
hygrometer	
quadrat	
ranging pole	

Table 2

Cambridge IGCSE Geography (0460) Paper 41, Q2b(i), June 2023

Data collection methods, fieldwork safety and equipment

Geographical enquiries require you to collect data. It is important to choose the right type of data so that it matches the aims of the investigation. Planning data collection methods requires an understanding of fieldwork safety and field equipment.

2   Students carried out fieldwork in their local town centre. They wanted to find out how successful the regeneration of the town centre had been.

The students decided to test the following hypotheses:

Hypothesis 1: Older people are happier with the regeneration than younger people.

Hypothesis 2: The regeneration has improved green spaces within the town centre.

Devise three suitable questions that the students could use in a questionnaire.

Sample student response	Commentary
1 Where do you live? 2 What is your name? 3 Do you like green spaces?	The first two questions are not needed to answer these hypotheses; in fact, questionnaires shouldn't ask for personal details like names at all. Question 3 is about green spaces, but it won't reveal whether the regeneration has improved green spaces within the town.
1 How old are you? 2 Do you like the regeneration that's taken place? 3 Do you visit green spaces?	The first question is very good. The second question is related to the hypotheses, but asking whether people 'like' the regeneration could get a different response than asking people if they are 'happy' with the regeneration, which is what Hypothesis 1 is about. Question 3 is irrelevant and does not help to answer either hypothesis.

Sample student response	Commentary
1 How old are you? 2 Are you happy about the regeneration that's taken place here? 3 Do you think the regeneration has improved green spaces within the town?	Questions 1 and 2 are focused and clear. They will help to answer Hypothesis 1. Question 3 is also clear and will help to answer Hypothesis 2.

Now try some more questions which test your knowledge about data collection methods, safety and field equipment.

3 **a** Students carried out some fieldwork about tourism at two sites near Kuala Lumpur, the capital city of Malaysia. The sites at Kuala Lumpur Bird Park and Batu Caves are shown in Figure 2.

Figure 2

The students decided to test the following hypotheses:

Hypothesis 1: More foreign tourists come from Southeast Asia than from other parts of the world.

Hypothesis 2: Visitors to the Kuala Lumpur Bird Park spoil the environment more than visitors to the Batu Caves.

To test **Hypothesis 1** the students asked 100 visitors at the tourist sites which country they came from.

The students used a systematic sampling method to select people to question. Describe this method of sampling. [2]

b Why is sampling a useful fieldwork technique? [2]

Cambridge IGCSE Geography (0460) Paper 41, Q2a(i), a(ii), June 2024

4 Students did fieldwork on a local coastline. They investigated a variety of topics including longshore drift and coastal management.

The students agreed to test the following hypotheses:

Hypothesis 1: Longshore drift is occurring along the local coastline.

Hypothesis 2: Coastal defences have a positive impact on the local coastline.

To investigate Hypothesis 1: Longshore drift is occurring along the local coastline, some students used the fieldwork method described in Figure 3.

> **A fieldwork method to test Hypothesis 1**
>
> - Use brightly coloured waterproof paint to paint 50 pebbles of different shapes and sizes.
>
> - Select a clear section of beach avoiding obstacles and groynes.
>
> - Put the pebbles in the zone of swash and backwash and mark the position of the pebbles with a ranging pole.
>
> - After one hour find the pebbles and work out the direction and distance that they have moved from the ranging pole.
>
> - Collect the pebbles to use them again. Replace any missing pebbles with spare ones.
>
> - Repeat the method three times.

Figure 3

Suggest why the students:

- painted the pebbles

- repeated their method three times.   [2]

Cambridge IGCSE Geography (0460) Paper 42, Q1b(i), March 2024

5   When conducting fieldwork in an urban area, students identified several potential risks shown in Table 3. Suggest one precaution that the students could take to reduce each possible risk.   [2]

Possible risk	Possible precaution
getting lost	
being run over by vehicles	

Table 3

6   How are ranging poles used in geography fieldwork?   [3]

7   a   Students were planning fieldwork on a local beach. This is shown in Figure 4. The beach has groynes which go from the back of the beach towards the sea.

Figure 4

Before the students began their fieldwork, their teacher reminded them of the safety precautions they must take.

Table 4 shows four possible dangerous situations. Suggest one different precaution that the students could take to reduce **each** possible danger. [4]

Possible danger	Possible precaution
Heavy rain is forecast on the day of the fieldwork.	
High cliffs at the back of the beach.	
Powerful waves break onto the beach.	
The beach is covered by the sea at high tide.	

Table 4

Cambridge IGCSE Geography (0460) Paper 42, Q1a November 2023

In Paper 4, there are often short questions that check how well you understand the topic. Knowing your topic well also means you can write sensible hypotheses and understand the aims of your fieldwork more clearly. It is therefore important to know your fieldwork topic well when doing your planning.

b Describe the beach shown in Figure 4. [2]

Cambridge IGCSE Geography (0460) Paper 42, Q1b, November 2023

Presenting and analysing data, and making conclusions

There are many ways to present data, and it is important to choose the right presentation technique. Analysing data involves looking for patterns and trends, and conclusions are reasoned judgements that use data to support them. Making conclusions also requires revisiting the hypotheses that you set out at the start of the investigation. The questions in this section test your understanding of presenting and analysing data and making conclusions.

8 Students have collected data on different types of land use (e.g. residential, commercial, industrial, recreational) along a transect from the centre of a town to its outskirts.

Suggest a method to present this information clearly and effectively. [4]

Sample student response	Commentary
I would use a bar chart to show the land use types.	This answer is too simplistic. Bar charts are a good idea, but it isn't clear whether the candidate is intending to draw more than one bar chart. As this data is taken along a transect, more than one bar chart needs to be drawn.
I would do a pie chart, showing the different land uses across the transect. To do this, I would add up all the land uses at all the sites and turn them into percentages. My pie chart would then summarise these percentages.	This answer has more detail, and pie charts are useful when showing percentages. However, this student intends to add up the land uses at all sites – this only tells us the overall land use in the city, and not how the land use changes across the transect.
I would draw a land use transect diagram, with the horizontal axis showing distance from the town centre and coloured bands representing different land uses at specific sites along the route. This allows clear visual comparison of how land use zones change with distance, making it easy to identify patterns such as the transition from commercial to residential areas.	This answer is good as it uses an appropriate method of presentation with each site displayed separately. There is a strong explanation of why the method is effective for showing change and comparison. Finally, the use of colours will help with clarity.

Now try some more questions which test your knowledge about presenting and analysing data and making conclusions.

9 a   Students did fieldwork on a local coastline. They investigated a variety of topics including longshore drift and coastal management.

The students agreed to test the following hypotheses:

Hypothesis 1: Longshore drift is occurring along the local coastline.

Hypothesis 2: Coastal defences have a positive impact on the local coastline.

The results of the students' measurements are shown in Table 5.

On a copy of Figure 5, **plot the results** of the total number of pebbles found and the average length of pebble that moved between 40.1 m and 50 m from the ranging pole (see PPQ 9a in the Resource Sheets).   [2]

Cambridge IGCSE Geography (0460) Paper 42, Q1b(ii) March 2024

Distance moved east from ranging pole (m)	Total number of pebbles found in the three tests	Average length of long axis of pebbles (cm)
0.1 to 10	4	8.5
10.1 to 20	15	7.2
20.1 to 30	24	6.6
30.1 to 40	33	5.7
40.1 to 50	**21**	**5.5**
50.1 to 60	17	5.1
60.1 to 70	13	4.3
70.1 to 80	9	4.0
more than 80	3	3.4

Table 5

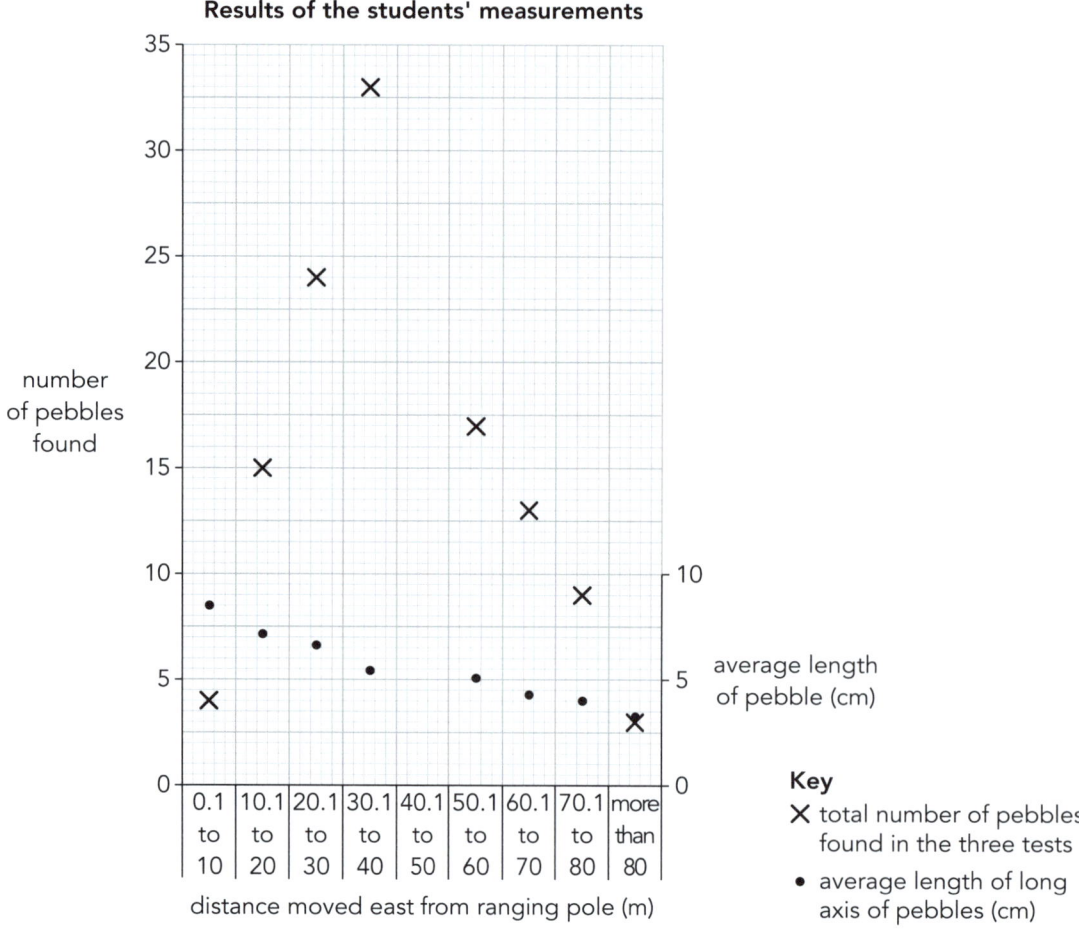

Figure 5

b Do the results shown in Figure 5 and Table 5 support Hypothesis 1: Longshore drift is occurring along the local coastline? Use data to support your conclusion. [4]

Cambridge IGCSE Geography (0460) Paper 42, Q1b(iii), March 2024

10 a Students did fieldwork on Ubin island, a small island between Malaysia and Singapore. Ubin is a rural area with little economic development. There has been much local discussion about whether the island should be protected from future development.

The students did their fieldwork at 20 sites on the eastern side of the island near to the main village.

They decided to investigate the following hypotheses:

Hypothesis 1: Environmental quality increases away from the village.

Hypothesis 2: Economic development on the island would bring more benefits than problems for local people.

To investigate **Hypothesis 1** one student completed a bi-polar survey on environmental quality at the different sites. The survey sheet is shown in Figure 6.

Site number:	Score					
Positive description	+2	+1	0	−1	−2	Negative description
beautiful landscape						ugly landscape
unspoilt by human activity, e.g. no litter						human activity spoils the landscape, e.g. litter
varied types of scenery						no variety of scenery
safe and appealing						unsafe and hostile
peaceful						noisy
human development fits in with the natural environment						development by people does not fit in with the natural environment

Total environmental quality score:

Figure 6

Suggest how the students could make sure that their bi-polar survey results are reliable.

Adapted from Cambridge IGCSE Geography (0460) Paper 42, Q2b(ii), June 2022

b   Table 6 shows Student A's results of the bi-polar survey for the 20 fieldwork sites.

Site number	Attractiveness of landscape	Result of human activity	Variation of scenery	Safety and appeal	Noise level	Sensitivity of human development	Total environmental quality score for site
1	0	−1	0	+1	+1	0	+1
2	−2	−1	−1	0	+1	+1	−2
3	−1	−1	0	0	−1	0	−3
4	+1	−1	0	+1	+1	+1	+3
5	0	−1	0	0	+1	0	0
6	+1	0	+2	+1	+1	0	+5
7	0	0	0	+1	0	0	+1
8	+2	+1	+2	+1	+1	+1	+8
9	0	0	0	+1	+1	+1	+3
10	0	0	−1	0	+1	0	0
11	0	0	−1	−1	0	0	−2
12	+1	0	+1	+2	+1	+1	+6
13	0	−1	−1	0	0	+1	−1
14	−2	0	−2	−1	0	−1	−6
15	−1	−1	−1	−1	0	+1	−3
16	+1	0	+1	+1	+2	+2	+7
17	0	0	−1	−1	0	0	−2
18	+1	−2	+1	+1	+1	+1	+3
19	+2	+1	+1	+2	+2	+2	+10
20	+2	−2	+1	−1	+1	0	+1
Total score across all sites	+5	−9	+1	+7	+14	+11	

Table 6

Which site has the lowest total environmental quality score?   [1]

Cambridge IGCSE Geography (0460) Paper 42, Q2c(i) June 2022

c   On a copy of Figure 7, plot the total environmental quality score for Sites 15 and 16 (see PPQ 10c in the Resource Sheets).   [2]

Total environmental quality scores at 20 fieldwork sites

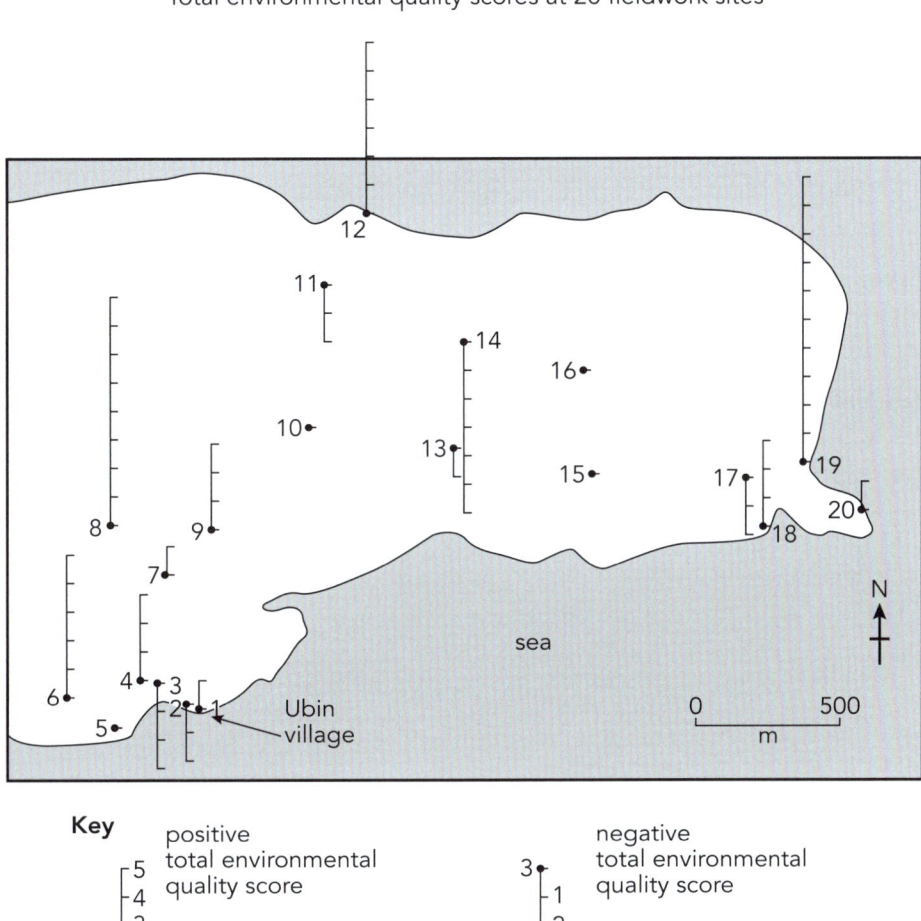

Figure 7

Adapted from Cambridge IGCSE Geography (0460) Paper 42, Q2c(iii), June 2022

d Estimate the distance between the two sites with the highest total environmental quality score (Sites 8 and 19).

Choose the best estimate from the options below:

i 500 km

ii 1000 km

iii 1500 km

iv 2200 km   [1]

This part of the question is author-written

11 a   A group of students visited Jwaneng, a large open-pit diamond mine in Botswana, an MIC in Africa. Most mining is done by blasting at or near the surface.

The students tested the following hypotheses:

Hypothesis 1: Employment is the most important benefit of the mine for residents of Jwaneng.

Hypothesis 2: The level of pollution increases towards the mine.

To investigate **Hypothesis 1** the students used a questionnaire with 100 local residents to study the impacts of Jwaneng mine. This questionnaire is shown in Figure 8.

Resident questionnaire

We are doing a survey about the local mine as part of our Geography fieldwork. Please will you answer the following questions?

1.   What do you think are the benefits of Jwaneng mine?

....

....

....

....

2.   What do you think are the disadvantages of Jwaneng mine?

....

....

....

....

Thank you for your time.

Figure 8

The results of Question 1 (What do you think are the benefits of Jwaneng mine?) are shown in Table 7. Use this data to **complete Figure 9** (see PPQ 11a in the Resource Sheets).   [2]

Benefits of the mine	Number of answers
employment	76
medical facilities	44
shops	30
education facilities	32
recreation facilities	20
aeroplane runway and roads	15

Table 7

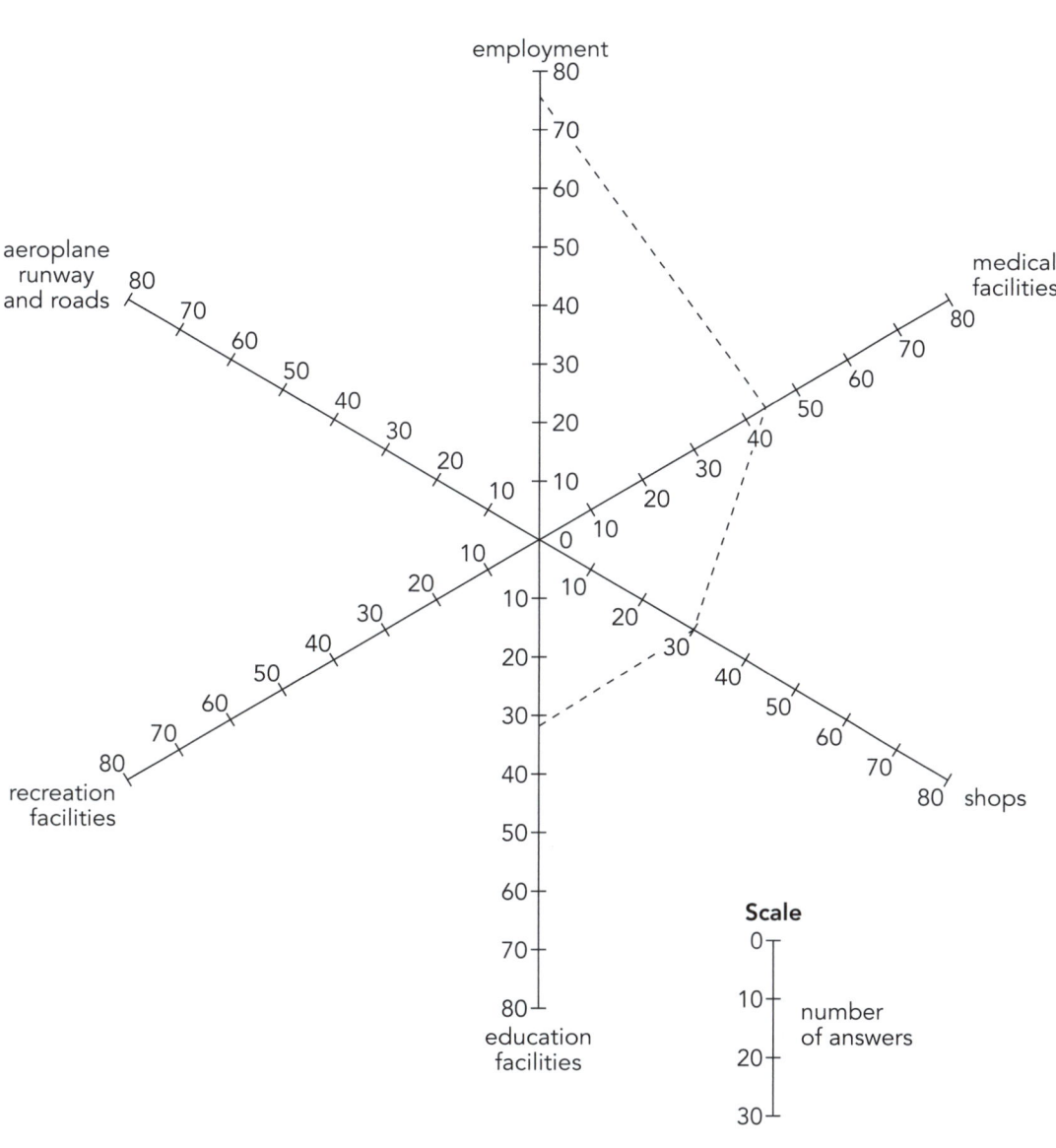

Benefits of the mine

Figure 9

Adapted from Cambridge IGCSE Geography (0460) Paper 41, Q1c(iii), November 2022

 b What conclusion did the students make to **Hypothesis 1:** Employment is the most important benefit of the mine for residents of Jwaneng? Support your answer with data from Figure 9 and Table 7. [3]

Cambridge IGCSE Geography (0460) Paper 41, Q1c(iv), November 2022

> Acknowledgements

The authors and publishers acknowledge the following sources of copyright material and are grateful for the permissions granted. While every effort has been made, it has not always been possible to identify the sources of all the material used, or to trace all copyright holders. If any omissions are brought to our notice, we will be happy to include the appropriate acknowledgements on reprinting.

Cambridge International Education copyright material in this publication is reproduced under license and remains the intellectual property of Cambridge University Press & Assessment.

Cambridge International Education bears no responsibility for the example answers to questions taken from its past question papers which are contained in this publication.

Thanks to the following for permission to reproduce images:

Cover Juan Maria Coy Vergara/Getty Images

Inside **Topic 1** LeilaSpb/GI; Figure 1.4 & 1.5 © Crown copyright and database rights 2024 OS Licence 100035409; **Topic 2** Tim Grist Photography/GI; @ Didier Marti/GI; Figure 2.3 Global distribution of tropical coral reefs (map data © 2019 Google). Locations provided by ReefBase (www.reefbase.org, last access: 16 July 2018), Jackson, Rebecca & Gabric, Albert & Cropp, Roger & Woodhouse, Matthew. (2020). Dimethylsulfide (DMS), marine biogenic aerosols and the ecophysiology of coral reefs. Biogeosciences. 17. 2181-2204. 10.5194/bg-17-2181-2020; **Topic 3** Wolfgang Kaehler/GI; Brandon Rosenblum/GI; Mark Newman/ GI; Auscape/GI; **Topic 4** Kriswanto Ginting/GI; Egon69/GI; **Topic 5** Alexandre Morin-Laprise/GI; Figure 5.2 Source: Temperature, NASA; Figure 5.3 © Bureau of Meteorology; **Exam Practice 1** Figure 1 & 11 Adapted Map of Earthquakes Global Overview (1 January - 5 June 2019) © European Union, 2019; Figure 3 Adapted Map of eruption of Mauna Loa from University of Hawai'I, used with the permission of Professor Kenna Rubin; Stephen J. Sibley; Manfred Gottschalk/GI; **Topic 8** FatCamera/GI; Sturti/ GI; **Topic 9** Bloomberg/GI; Figure 9.4 © Crown copyright and database rights 2024 OS Licence 100035409; Luis Davilla/GI; Jose A. Bernat Bacete/GI; **Topic 10** Figure 10.2 Daily supply of calories per person, 2018, OurWorldInData.org/food-supply CC BY, Data source: Food and Agriculture Organization of the United Nations (2023) and other sources; **Exam Practice 2** Stephen J. Sibley; Figure 12 plotly.com; Figure 15 based on a map from Servicio Nacional de Geología y Minería - Gobierno de Chile; Fig 17 based on original graphic by The World Bank; Daily supply of calories per person, 2018, OurWorldInData.org/food-supply CC BY, Data source: Food and Agriculture Organization of the United Nations (2023) and other sources; Figure 20 Max Roser (2023) "Demographic transition: Why is rapid population growth a temporary phenomenon?" Published online at OurWorldInData.org. Retrieved from: https://ourworldindata.org/demographic-transition; Population density map of Europe from Eurostat. European Commission (Eurostat, Joint Research Centre and DG Regional Policy - REGIO-GIS); **Exam Practice 3** Robertharding/Alamy Stock Photo; Christian Kober 1/Alamy Stock Photo; © David Dixon CC-BY-SA

Flip card 1 James Osmond/GI; **Flip card 2** Ashley Cooper/GI; Owngarden/GI

MCQ 1 LeliaSpb/GI; Astromujoff/GI; **MCQ 6** © 2023 by PopulationPyramid.net under Creative Commons license CC BY 3.0 IGO

Key GI = Getty Images